THE ROAD TO SUCCESS

A Practical Handbook for Development Practitioners (The NGO Perspective)

Yusto Paradius Muchuruza, PhD

TANZANIA EDUCATIONAL PUBLISHERS LTD

Tanzania Educational Publishers Ltd,
TEPU House,
Uganda Road, Plot No. 45 Block MDA,
Mob: +255 685 997583/ +255 758 147871
Email: tepultd@yahoo.com
Website: www.tepu.co.tz
P.O. Box 1222,
Bukoba, Tanzania.

ISBN 978 9987 07 012 1

DEDICATION

I dedicate this book to all NGO Founders, Workers, Managers, Beneficiaries, Social Development Trainers, Development Practioners and Stakeholders.

I also dedicate it to my loved wife, Rose Kokuhumbya and our beloved children:

Lilian Kokugonza

Albert Lugazia

Augustina Kokutona

Geoffrey Njunwa

Elieth Kokumanya

Editha Owokusima

TABLE OF CONTENTS

LIST ABBREVIATIONS AND ACRONYMS

AU	-	African Union
BaU	-	Business as Usual
CBO	-	Community Based Organizations
CEO	-	Chief Executive Officer
CSOs	-	Civil Society Organizations
ESAURP	-	East and South African Universities Research Programme
ESCE	-	Economic, Social, Cultural and Environmental Development
ETC	-	Et cetra (and so on)
FBOs	-	Faith Based Organizations
HR	-	Human Resource
HRM	-	Human Resource Management
HRM	-	Human Resource Manager
HRMD	-	Human Resource Management Department
INGOs	-	International Non-Governmental Organizations
KADETFU	-	Kagera Development and Credit Revolving Fund
NGO	-	None Governmental Organization
NPOs	-	Non-Political Organizations

NSAs	-	Non-State Actors
OD	-	Organizational Development
OM	-	Organizational Management
PEST	-	Political, Economic, Social and Technological
SMART	-	Specific, Measurable, Attainable, Results oriented/Realistic, Time bound
SWOT	-	Strength, Weakness, Opportunities, Threats
UN	-	United Nations
URT	-	United Republic of Tanzania
USA	-	United States of America

FOREWORD

During the last decade, one of the significant achievements on the growth chart of the civil society in Tanzania was its recognition by the governments for what it truly is, a means through which the participation of citizens in governance processes and development arena can be achieved. We have seen stronger organizations arising from communities, with enhanced ability to meet bigger challenges and achieving better outcomes. Gone are the days when local civil society organizations (CSOs) were perceived to be lacking in capacity and experience to effectively implement projects. We are now seeing a big shift and movement within civil society organizations sector. Most of civil society organizations are growing and becoming stronger and their roles and mission are becoming clearer. They are working in diverse issues and exhibiting good professional expertise in their areas of work. Without doubt, the civil society organizations are agents for change in our communities.

Non-Governmental Organizations (NGOs) are one of the change agents as far as community development is concerned; thus, investing direct resources into them is a viable strategy for community transformation and change. Being a part of CSOs, NGOs are among the most important and potent forces for economic, social, cultural and environmental development. They are imperative partners in the development process of any nation. NGOs complement governments' efforts towards transforming the social wellbeing of the people. They make a difference in the lives of many people as they supplement public institutions by providing human needs that are not adequately covered by the institutions.

Increasingly the governments are now recognizing NGOs as partners in the development process. Hence it is expected that the governments will put in place and create an enabling environment for the NGOs to work effectively and efficiently for the development of the countries concerned. Evidence on ground show that most of CSOs are getting sufficient support from their governments which is an indication that they trust and appreciate their contribution in improving people's lives in communities.

On the other hand, many NGOs have been formed in many countries, yet few are sustainable and resilient to survive challenging times. They still face many problems. The challenge for their future is to recognize their weaknesses and strategically address them. However, the main reason for the demise of many NGOs has been the fact that most Development Practitioners (founders, managers and workers) have inadequate or no skills in the management of institutions of such nature, this is due to the lack of a resource-book.

Fortunately, the author, Dr. Yusto Muchuruza, a social scientist and proficient worker, with experience and expertise in social development and organizational management, a facilitator and an experienced Development Practitioner has written this "Practical Handbook for Development Practitioners – The NGOs Perspective." This book represents a modest attempt to build the organizational capacity of the civil society in Tanzania and beyond. It represents a body of knowledge and skills required by Development Practitioners to effectively carry out their duties and responsibilities, and finally achieve organizational goals.

With that in mind, I congratulate Dr. Yusto Paradius Muchuruza for writing this handbook. I have read it and found it to be a helpful resource for all organizations; NGOs founders, practitioners, leaders, and other development stakeholders.

For this reason, I recommend it to all Non-Governmental Organizations, Governmental Organizations and Governments, to sustain the civil society sector's eagerness and commitment to seize their roles in mobilizing citizens for development at the local, national and international levels.

Francis Kiwanga,
Executive Director,
The Foundation for Civil Society
Dar es Salaam
Tanzania.
October 2020

INTRODUCTION

The NGOs Sector Has Been My Road to Success

When I was young, throughout my years in school, my ambition was to become a community worker to serve the community I lived in. I could see how my parents were struggling to pay school fees and other needs for me and my siblings, pay medical fees when I and my relatives were sick, the type of water we used to drink and the general living standard of our community. This motivated me to do something to reverse the situation.

After completing my secondary school education, I was employed by Ndolage Mission Hospital as a Ward Attendant. I didn't want to go for higher education because I wanted to support my young brothers and sisters in education. So, I thought, if I start working, the small earnings I get, will support both me and my family.

While working at that Hospital, I was lucky to be selected to join a choir which was invited to visit Germany. In the latter, I found life was quite different from the living standard I was used to in my community. On my return, I decided to go for more studies with hope that if I obtain a higher education, I'll definitely get another chance to visit Europe and even find a job there.

Some years later, I took studies to be a Medical Laboratory Technician and upon graduation got employed at the same hospital. However, because this could not give me a chance to visit Europe again, I decided to change the field and went for studies in Masonry and House Building, Electrical Installation and Plumbing. Lucky enough, I returned to the same Hospital and got re-employed as a Technician dealing with minor repairs in plumbing, electricity, houses and even through experience, repairing hospital cars. Again, this work could not give me chance to visit Europe again though I was working with the European Missionaries, like Dr. Rune Grenholm from

Sweden, Engineer Goran Frisk from Sweden as well as other Missionaries from German and Denmark.

After some years in the same work, I decided to change again and became a politician. This is because I saw politicians were well off in terms of living standards. I went for a political course at Murutunguru Political Institute in Tanzania. I didn't do much in politics, partly because this cadre was completely disconnected with my ambition of working for my community or visit and/or live in Europe/USA.

Later, I decided to join an NGO called "Walio katika Mapambano na AIDS Tanzania" (WAMATA), literally meaning "Those in fight against AIDS in Tanzania" and later joined Kagera Development and Credit Revolving Fund (KADETFU), where I am working until now.

With and through the NGO sector, my future become promising. I was often invited to meetings and workshops inside and outside my country and these safari (trips) gave me money in terms of DSA and travelling allowances. I could use flights every time and therefore became more familiar with many parts of the world.

While working in the NGOs sector, I got opportunities to go for more studies in and outside the country. I went out and came back to work for my community. The NGOs sector, however, gave me more opportunities including studying and eventually being awarded a Doctorate of Humanities. Really, the NGO sector has been **"My Road to Success."**

Yusto P. Muchuruza,
Bukoba, Tanzania
August, 2020

ACKNOWLEDGEMENT

First and foremost, I would like to express my gratitude to Almighty God for enabling me to carry out this task of writing a book. Sometimes I felt weak and despaired, but my God strengthened me until I gained new courage. Without thy guidance, I would not have managed to accomplish this work.

Secondly, I wish to express my special gratitude and love to my wife Rose Kokuhumbya, who at all times, encouraged me to continue with this task. Her question was always: "When will you accomplish this work?" Thank you, my beloved wife.

Also, our children Lilian, Albert, Augustina, Geoffrey and Dr. Elieth, were among the well-wishers through their encouragement and tolerance during the whole period when I kept in my library writing this book. Sometimes, I used the family time to work on this book. They all deserve my admiration.

I wish also to convey my gratitude to the Editors of Tanzania Educational Publishers Ltd, who edited this book and published it.

I can't forget my colleagues at KADETFU, the organization which gave me acquiescence to work on this book that focuses on its vision, mission and goals.

Finally, it is obvious that; the base of my knowledge and skills is the training I got from The Institute of Cultural Affairs (ICA) in Brussels, Belgium in 1994. This training was an eye opener on the development arena. My instructor Dr. Jim Campbell and his team will remain in my mind and prayers, for many years to come. To make me complete in this field, the East and

South African Universities Research Programme (ESAURP) cemented what I had obtained from ICA in NGO management. My gratitude should, therefore, reach both ICA and ESAURP for preparing me for this work. This book is a result of their work.

Yusto Paradius Muchuruza
Bukoba, Tanzania.
August, 2020

ABOUT THE AUTHOR AND THE BOOK

ABOUT THE AUTHOR

Dr. Yusto Paradius Muchuruza was born in 1954 at Bushagara Village, Muleba District, Kagera Region, Tanzania. He is a social scientist with qualifications and experience in social development and organizational management. He attended various courses and trainings in the social development arena including qualifications in MA-Sociology (AU-USA), Diploma in Organizational Finance and Project Management, (Institute of Cultural Affairs, (ICA) Brussels, Belgium) and Advanced Diploma in Land Management and Informal Settlement Regularization (Erasmus University- IHS, Rotterdam, The Netherlands).

Other qualifications include; Advanced Diploma in Leadership Development; (St. Francis Xavier University, COADY International Institute), Nova Scotia, Canada, Diploma in Managing Community Based Projects, (Makerere University, Kampala, Uganda) and many other formal and informal short courses and trainings comprising Certificates in Facilitation skills, Participatory Planning in Development, (PPD) (ICA, Brussels, Belgium), Certificate of NGO Management (Organized by ESAURP) Dar es Salaam, Tanzania, Certificate in International Human Rights Training Programme" (IHRTP) (Sainte-Anne-de-Bellevue University, in Montreal, Canada), Certificate in Technology of Participation (ToP) (ICA, Brussels, Belgium) and Financial Management for donor funded projects. Dr. Yusto Paradius Muchuruza is a holder of a Doctorate of Humanities from the Commonwealth University in the UK.

Dr. Muchuruza is a proficient social worker, a Facilitator and an experienced Development Practitioner. He participated and/or conducted various researches and evaluation workouts. He has written many books and presented papers at local and international forums, conferences and workshops. He is currently the Executive Director of a renowned and triumphant Tanzanian NGO known as Kagera Development and Credit Revolving Fund (KADETFU), (www.kadetfu.or.tz), the organization that won many awards under his leadership such as: the Lake Victoria Environmental Award, the Tanzania CSOs Excellence Award, the Best Grantee Award, the Knowledge Brokering, Networking and Marketing Award, the Certificate of Merit and two East African Fisheries Awards.

Dr. Muchuruza is a member of the Regional Advisory Committee of the Open University of Tanzania, Kagera Center. He is also Chair/and or member of many local and international Programmes/Project Steering Committees (PSCs) and Management Boards including; Open University Advisory Board, Nile Basin Initiative (NBI), NOSOLIDECO, SASEDO, TADEPA, LAVNET, Bujugo Secondary School, ELCT/NWD Synodal Council and the Kagera Regional Tourism Committee, to mention a few.

He is the author of many publications, which include the following:

1. *Shaping the Future of Africa (1998): Historical Background in Political, Economic, and Cultural Commonalities, Influencing the Direction of African Development.*

2. *Karibu Bukoba (2002): The Guide for Visitors to Kagera Region.*

3. *Sheria na Mikataba ya Kimataifa Kuhusu Haki za Watoto (2004)*

4. *I believe (2011): The Study on the Human Rights Universality versus Traditions.*

5. *Uongozi wa Kiroho: Misingi ya Uongozi katika Kanisa la Kikristo (2020)*

6. *Research Report: The Effects of BXW on Food Security and the Peoples Livelihood (2013)*

ABOUT THIS BOOK

Most of the Development Practitioners, especially the NGO/CSO workers, have inadequate or with no skills in their work as NGO/CSO managers or workers. They have been motivated by the situation, and sometimes some people after retirement from their jobs do join the NGO sector for the purpose of serving the community or having something to do after retirement. Most NGO leaders and managers have qualifications as medical personnel, teachers, engineers, politicians etc, the skills which have no connection with NGO management.

This book aims at providing NGO workers, social development trainers and all Development Practitioners with knowledge and ability to run their organizations and/or exchange experience in different fields of social development. It is a Practical reference for Handbook for Development Practitioners while at work or during staff development programmes.

This book has thirteen chapters which are as follows:

Chapter One explains in broad terms the definition of Organization, Kinds of Organizations and the Meaning of Non-Governmental Organizations (NGOs). The chapter also shades light on the ways and procedures of how to start an NGO taking examples from different countries. It gives light on the lawful procedures for Establishment and Registration of NGOs and what is needed to ensure Organizational Effectiveness.

Chapter Two deals with Project Design, Implementation and Management. It defines the term "Project," giving an overview on the NGO projects as distinguished from other projects. It also explains the NGO Roles in the Project Cycle, Project Management and the Steps of Project Management.

Chapter Three elucidates on Fund Raising and Resource Mobilization definitions including the types of Fund-Raising Strategies and Methods (Source of Funds).

Chapter Four is about Writing a Project Proposal and its definition, Project Proposal Formats and types.

Chapter Five clarifies on the Key Elements/Sections of a Standard Project Proposal, Guidelines for Writing a Generic/ Standard Proposal and a Logical Flow of a Generic/Standard Project Proposal.

Chapter Six is about Monitoring and Evaluation, citing on the Project Monitoring and Evaluation definitions and procedures.

Chapter Seven gives light on the Project Output, Outcome and Impact. It also cites on the Project Sustainability/Future Funding, Project Budget and other elements of a project proposal such as Annexes/Appendices and the Covering Letter.

Chapter Eight is all about How to Assess the Viable Project Proposal. This tool is normally used by the funding agent to assess if the project meets their funding requirements.

Chapter Nine is about Writing the Project Report. It defines what is a Project Report, Stages of Project Report Writing and the Ten Steps involved in Report Writing.

Chapter Ten of this book is on Recommendations on How to Approach and Win a Donor.

Chapter Eleven clarifies about Financial Management, Financial Sustainability and Financial Wealth within an organization. The chapter also explains on how to Maintain Financial Flow in the organization using different financial sustainability approaches. The chapter includes the Accounting System, the Organization Budget and Budgeting and the Cash Flow.

Chapter Twelve describes Organizational Management (OM), Organization Effectiveness, Management Characteristics of NGO Managers, Organizational Functions, Obstacles to effective Organizational Management, Development principles in Organizational Management and Community Participation as a tool for effective Management.

Chapter Thirteen explains Human Resource Management (HRM) and its definition, What does workers bring to the organization, Making the most use of what workers bring to the organization, Assessing the organization workers as assets and Human Resource Development (HRD) for organizational growth.

The book, further encompasses tables and figures to help the readers understand what can be done by Development Practitioners for their organizational effectiveness.

It ends up with References and Links.

CHAPTER ONE

THE ORGANIZATION

1.1 Definition of "Organization"

An organization is an organized group (or team) of people who have joined together to achieve a common goal or purpose. The word "organization" is derived from the Greek word *organon*, which means tool or instrument, musical instrument and organ.

There are four key words in the above definition of the word "Organization." The first is *"pur-pose"* – this means; an organization must have a clearly-defined drive or determination, smart goals and practical strategies. The second word is *"people"*: the individual members of staff with relevant expertise and commitment to the organization. These are also known as Human Resources.

The third key word is *"organized"* which, in management terms, can be represented by the structure, systems and administrative purposes. Finally, there is the concept of the *"group"* – this means, people must work together in team work as an integrated and effective squad.

On the other hand, organization can be defined as an action that means *"organizing."* This is the process of defining and grouping the activities of the organization and establishing the authority relationships among them.

Arthita Banerjee defines the Organization as "the determination and assignment of duties of people, and also the establishment and the maintenance of authority relationship among these grouped activities. Organization is the structural framework within which the various efforts are coordinated and relate to each other" *http://www. preservearticles.com/meaning/what-is-the-definition-of-the-term-organisation/29653*

1.2 Kinds of Organizations

1.2.1 Organizational Development

Meaning of "Development"

Development is transformation and advancement of people from one level or standard of living to a better one. Transformation should aim at developing the whole human being; promoting his/her advancement socially, economically, spiritually, culturally and politically.

Development must, therefore, aim at transforming people's livelihoods. Development of properties, assets and infrastructures, are catalysts to the same, they should aim at transforming livelihood of people. Meaningful development of "things" must enhance development of the people and their environment.

Nyerere J.K. (1974) put it like this; "For the truth is that development means the development of people. Roads, buildings, increase of crop output and other things of this nature, are not development; they are only tools for development" *(Nyerere, J.K.,1974, - Man and Development).*

One can make development of his/her family or him/her self, right; this is also development, but since it benefits just individuals, it is not a complete development, it is a family gain.

Nyerere, J.K. (1974), further insists that "A man develops himself by joining in free discussion of a new venture and participating in the subsequent decision; he is not being developed if he is herded like an animal into the new pastures. Development of man can, in fact, only be effected by that man; development of the people can only be effected by the people" *(Nyerere, J.K. 1974, Man and Development).*

The work of all development practitioners, duty bearers and service providers, including, Local Government Authorities, CSOs, NGOs, Faith Organizations, the private sector, Cooperatives and other non-state actors; aims at bringing about development of people. However; if this development is not a free development and does not result into well-being of people, it is "a forced development" and it cannot benefit the people. The proverb that is common in the social arena: *"you can drive a donkey to water, but you cannot force it drink that water"*, illustrates the importance of involving people in cultivation of their own development.

Nyerere, J.K. (1974) commented on this; "Development brings freedom, provided it is development of people. But people cannot be developed, they can only develop themselves" *(Nyerere, J.K., 1974; Man, and Development)*

Meaningful development is the process of transforming people economically, socially, culturally and even psychologically. The Business Dictionary defines the term *"development"* as "the process of economic and social transformation that is based on complex cultural and environmental factors and their interactions." Source: *(http://www.businessdictionary.com/ definition/development.html*

Organizational Development can be easily termed literary as a growing process of an organization in terms of human, financial and material resources and their management.

Logically, OD is a field of investigation or research, hypothesis and practice dedicated to intensifying people's knowledge and effectiveness to accomplish more successful organizational change and performance.

Carrie Foster 2014, emphasizes that OD has its foundations in a number of behavioral and social sciences and OD practitioners are unashamedly humanistic in their approach to change management and delivering sustainable organizational performance. *Carrie Foster 2014, (Organization Development Practitioner; Consultant; Facilitator; Coach).*

Francis et al 2012, defines OD as "both the field of applied behavioral science focused on understanding and managing organizational change to increase an organization's effectiveness and viability and a field of scientific study and enquiry" *Francis et al 2012, (Creating Sense of Community: The role of public space).*

Most of the organizations don't see OD as a tool for transformational change. They don't put emphasis in investing to their programmes or development interventions; as a result, they fail to achieve their goals.

Francis et al (2012), further insists that; "Organization Development believes that every part of an organization is integral to a system that relies on and impacts other elements of the internal and external environment in which the organization operates. OD helps organizations to deliver sustainable performance improvement through people. Those who practice OD usually have a strong humanistic and democratic approach to organizational change" *(Francis et al, 2012, (Creating Sense of Community: The role of public space.*

When participatory methods are used with involvement of people, they remain key features of OD interventions. A Development Practitioner will get involved in a number of holistic OD interventions partly or fully as the case may be, including; organization diagnostic, strategic thinking, culture change, change management, coaching, mentoring, leadership development, team building, organizational design, monitoring and evaluation, performance management and assessment, talent management, HR processes including learning and development, to mention a few.

For positive organizational change that brings sustainable development, a number of organizational development strategies should be put in place to deliver applicable effective performance and its required outcomes.

This analysis implies that Organizational Development should become a major component in management training programmes, because, most efforts to improve organizational effectiveness are initiated and carried out by the staff themselves, without external help.

However, at the same time, the NGO community needs access to trained and experienced OD consultants, people who understand NGOs and know how to facilitate and support the organization's own efforts to identify problems and opportunities.

In the development field, consultants are too often seen as donor –imposed evaluators, either of the organization or of its programmes. The OD consultant, on the contrary, works solely for the organization and can be an extremely useful tool in helping the organization to implement strategies designed to resolve blockages and, in general, to strengthen itself through, for example, strategic management and team-building. *(Campbell P, 1988-Editorial).*

1.2.2 Development Organizations

While OD is a logical process to the growth of an organization, Development Organization (DO) is a result that comes out as a consequence of OD interventions. This means, an organization cannot develop without first putting in place OD procedures and its implementation strategies. Development organization is therefore different from Organizational Development.

There are many groups, organizations and movements designed and established to foster development initiatives. These include CSOs (CBOs, NGOs, FBOs, GDOs) INGOs, IGOs which are formed or established with the clear aim to foster development interventions and therefore become Development Organizations.

This book will mainly focus on Non-Governmental Organizations (NGOs) which is the main motivation of writing this book, although in some instances, it will touch other types of Development Organizations as samples.

1.3 Non-Governmental Organizations

1.3.1 NGOs are Change Agents for Community Development

NGOs are one of the main change agents as far as community development is concerned, thus; investing direct resources into them is a viable strategy for community transformation and change. Being part of CSOs, NGOs are the important and potent forces for economic, social, cultural and environmental (ESCE) development. They are imperative partners in the development process of any nation. NGOs reach where the government has not reached yet; they complement government's efforts towards transforming the social well-being of the people. They make a difference to the lives of many people as they fill the gaps in human needs that are not adequately covered by governments.

Whilst they are Non-State Actors (NSAs), NGOs are also recognized by governments as the right arm in the development arena and hence is expected to put in place and create an enabling environment for the NGOs to work effectively and efficiently in development of the country.

"In Tanzania, NGOs are recognized by the Government as important partners in nation building and national development; valuable forces in promoting the qualitative and quantitative development of democracy and not least, important contributors to GDP" *(URT 2002-NGO Policy 2002).*

1.3.2 Definition of a Non-Governmental Organization

A Non-Governmental Organization (NGO) is a citizen-based, non-profit making organization which is sovereign and operating independently of government cycles at grassroots level. Normally, NGOs' task is to deliver resources or services in social or political purposes such as promoting economy, social or cultural development, advocating for human rights and good governance or as community representatives through lobbying and advocacy.

In Tanzania, a Non-Governmental Organization (NGO) is defined by the law as "A voluntary grouping of individuals or organizations which is autonomous, non-partisan, non-profit making organized locally at the grassroots, national or international levels for the purpose of enhancing or promoting economy, environmental, social or cultural development or protecting environment, lobbying or advocating on issues of public interest of a group of individuals or organizations, and includes Non-Governmental organizations established under the auspicious of any religious organization or faith propagating organization, trade union, sports clubs, political party, or community based organization, but does not include a trade union, a social club or a sports club, a political party, a religious organization or a community based organization." *(URT, 2002; the Non-Governmental Organization Act 2002).*

The Global NGO Network defines a Non-Governmental Organization (NGO) as "Any non-profit, voluntary citizens' group which is organized on a local, national or international level. While they are task-oriented and driven by people with a common interest, NGOs perform a variety of service and humanitarian functions, bring citizen concerns to governments, advocate and monitor policies and encourage political participation through provision of information." *(Source: http://www.ngo.org/ngoinfo/define.html).*

World Bank classifies NGOs as either operational organizations, which are primarily concerned with development projects, or advocacy organizations, which are primarily concerned with promoting a cause.

Srinivas, H. 2015, commented that; "There are many classifications of NGO/NPOs as determined by individual country's laws and regulations, including co-operatives, credit unions, societies, people's organizations or community groups etc. The classifications can also designate NGO/NPOs as religious, charitable, educational, scientific, literary or other organizations. These organizations may qualify for income tax exemption or other financial benefits. Regional and local tax exemptions may also apply on a region by region, or country by country basis." *(Srinivas, H. (2015), – Starting an NGO, Management Tools Series E-52).*

Some NGOs, however, are organized around specific issues such as governance, poverty reduction, health, human rights, environment etc. Most of them provide expertise, studies and evaluations, early warning mechanisms and strategies, monitoring and implementation of international treaties and agreements.

All NGOs/NPOs and governments have one thing in common, they all focus on development of people. Therefore, since NGOs are key partners in development cycles of any community, nation, local or central governments, all development planners at any level should consider involving this sector as fundamental associates.

1.3.3 *Starting, Establishment and Registration of a Non-Governmental Organization*

Starting an NGO is like buying a new car, there is always much enthusiasm, hopes and expectations at the beginning on what will the new car bring about in the family. But, as the car gets old, the excitement decreases and lets the family members classify it as a family property. As the car needs servicing and maintenance to keep enthusiasm and expectations to the family, NGOs also need upholding and timely perpetuation through programme reformation, staff development, monitoring and evaluation and in the course of that, ownership becomes viable; thus, triggering commitment and loyalty among the staff, management and other stakeholders.

An NGO can be started and established by any person or group of persons with a development spirit and vision. However, the process involved, defers from country to country depending on the specific country's laws and policies. In some countries the process can be lengthy, time consuming and sometimes discouraging while in other countries the process takes just a short time.

Even though, the difficulties of the process can be minimized by following consistent series of steps and seeking advice when needed. In some countries, governments regard NGO establishment as a blessing because they complement their efforts towards developing its people in providing much needed services to their respective communities and thorough planning during the start-up process is crucial to developing an effective and professional organization that is able to meet the myriad challenges faced by the world today. Therefore, registering NGOs shouldn't be a complex process.

The simple way to minimize the complexities of the process is by first reading and understanding the law and policies of the specific country where the NGO establishment will take place. In most countries, there are responsible Ministries or specialized departments within the government authorities that deal with registration of NGOs. It is believed, however, that; in some countries, registration of NGOs may take a year or beyond and in some countries, refused number of NGO registration is bigger than those agreed while revocation of NGOs is a normal phenomenon in other countries.

On the registration stage, there are several documents that need to be submitted to the registering authority and these also differ from country to country. Such documents which are needed to be submitted to the appropriate authority for registering an NGO may include; a Constitution or Memorandum and Articles of Organization that consist of Articles explaining the name of a NGO, objectives, leadership structure and responsibilities, meetings schedules and powers, reporting procedures, financial management systems, sources of income and expenditure. Other documents might be; CVs of the Executive Board members, endorsement from local authorities (letters of support), minutes from the General Assembly (GA) signed by founder members, that endorses the establishment of the NGO etc.

1.3.4 Registration of NGOs in Tanzania

In Tanzania for instance, NGO registration process takes a short time, and needs only four documents i.e. the Constitution/ Articles of Memorandum, personal particulars of office bearers, Minutes of a General Assembly (GA) containing full names and signatures of founder members and a filled registration application form. With all needed documents, the registration can be obtained in less than 60 days.

According to the Tanzania Non-Governmental Organizations Act, No. 24 of 2002, Sections 22 (1) and 23 (1) (2) (3), there are different levels for registration of Non-Governmental Organizations in Tanzania. The lower level is the District, secondly the Region, and finally the National level that include registration for International NGOs. To wit this Law; Public Officers, the District Administrative Officer (DAS) and Regional Planning Officer (RPO); are appointed to facilitate registration at their respective levels.

Section 12 (2) of the above said Non-Governmental Organizations Act, registration of NGOs in Tanzania should be accompanied by the following:

i)   Copy of the Constitution.

ii)   Minutes containing full names and signatures of founder members.

iii) Personal particulars (CVs) of office bearers, namely; the Chairperson, Secretary, Treasurer and other anticipated top leaders of the NGO.

iv)   Physical Location and address of the head office of Non-Governmental Organization *(normally found in the constitution)*.

v)   Application fee shall be stipulated by the concern authority from time to time.

vi) All other documents and particulars that shall be required by the Registering Authority.

Additionally, NGOs that have been in existence before the establishment of the new law No. 24 of 2002, have to comply with this law and thus obtain the Certificate of Compliance of which its application need to be accompanied by the following documents:

i)   Copy of Constitution of the Non-Governmental Organization.

ii)   Registration Certificate of Incorporation.

iii) Minutes containing full names and signatures of founder members.

iv)   Curriculum Vitae (CV) and Personal particulars of office bearers.

v)   Physical location and Address of the current head office of the Non-Governmental Organization.

vi)   Any requirement that may be mandatory for compliance as shall be required by the Registrar.

Applications for both registration and Certificate of Compliance of Non-Governmental Organization shall be in the prescribed forms i.e. NGO A Form No. 1 and NGO A Form No. 3 respectively. *(URT 2002, - Non Governmental Organization-NGO Act 2002)*

1.3.5. NGO Registration Fees (the case of Tanzania)

It is obvious that Tanzania has conducive environment for NGOs registration and management. While other countries charge thousands of dollars to register NGOs, the Tanzania case is different.

Registration fees at the district level are only TZS 41,500/= (about US$ 18), being filing fees TZS 15,000/= (US$ 6.5), Registration fee TZS 25,000/= (US$ 11) and Stamp Duty fee TZS 1,500/= (US$ 0.6). *(These fees are subject to change).*

While Registration fees at the Regional level are only TZS 56,500/= (US$ 22.5), at the National level, fees are TZS 66,500/= (US$ 26) and for International NGOs, the registration fees are US$ 267.

Apart from the registration and Certificate of Compliance (CoC) fees; all registered NGOs ought to pay annual fees of TZS 50,000/= (US$ 20) or USD 60 for International NGOs. The law, however, provides a provision in which NGOs with Certificates of Compliance are required to pay annual fees after completion of one year since they obtained such Certificates.

Other requirements include among others; submission of Annual Activity Report and Annual Financial Audited Reports at the end of each calendar year. This is done using the prescribed form i.e. NGO A Form No. 10.

1.3.6 Registration of NGOs in Uganda

In Uganda, (the neighboring country to Tanzania) you need more than ten documents and registration can be obtained in between four and six months.

To verify this; **Anguilla, D. 2014**, noted that; "In Uganda the Non-Governmental Organizations are regulated by the Non-Governmental Organizations Registration Act, Cap 113 as amended in 2006. Registration of NGOs in Uganda is seen by many as a complex process given the time it takes and the documentation involved." *(Angualia, D. 2014 - Legal Requirements for Registration of NGOs in Uganda).*

When starting an NGO, there should be an idea of what the NGO is formed to serve. This idea has to come from the real situation or need found in the concerned community and the NGO is formed to provide relief of such situation.

Establishment and registration of NGOs differ from one country to another depending on the law and policies that govern and regulate registration and functions of NGOs within the specific country.

1.3.7 Registering an International NGO (INGO) in Tanzania

International NGOs are recognized by the law in Tanzania as charitable organizations. They should, however, have originally been registered in another country outside Tanzania. Procedures for registration of these INGOs in Tanzania is in accordance with the above-mentioned NGO Act No. 24 of 2002.

(a)The procedures for registration of INGOs in Tanzania includes:

i.   Submission of an application for registration that shall be dully filled on the prescribed Form No.1

ii. Application must be submitted by three or more founder members while the law insists that at least two members out of these founder members should be residents of Tanzania.

iii. Application should be submitted to the Registrar at National Level who will acknowledge receipt and give feedback of the application outcome thereof.

(b) The Application shall be accompanied by the following documents:

i. Certificate of incorporation from the Country of Origin as a proof of its existence as a charity, or the same has been registered in the Country of origin for charitable purposes;

ii. The governing Constitution/ by laws of the organization as per Section 30 of the NGO Act, which requires all NGOs to adhere to the terms stipulated under the Constitution which is the governing document;

iii. Minutes containing full names and particulars of founder members;

iv. Curriculum Vitae (CVs) and Personal Particulars of office bearers;

v. Address and physical location in Tanzania of the INGO of the proposed head office and/or branches;

vi. Bank pay in slip for the Application Fees that shall be paid in the government account.

vii. Any other information and requirements that shall be mandatory as directed by the Registrar of NGOs in Tanzania.

"International Non-Governmental Organizations (INGOs) are required to have a minimum number of three or more persons at the time of registration, however, the NGOs in Tanzania are member based and the number of members can increase based on the need of each organization. Once all of the above requisite requirements are met under the Act, the Registrar will register the INGO and issue a certificate of registration". *(URT 2004 – NGO Act 2002)* http://vemmaattorneys.co.tz/2016/04/12/procedures-registering-international-ngos-tanzania/).

1.3.8 Registration of NGOs in India

In India; NGOs are registered in three categories, the Trust, Society and Non-profit companies.

- **Trusts:** The public charitable trust is a possible form of not-for-profit entity in India. Typically, public charitable trusts can be established for a number of purposes, including the relief of poverty, education, medical, provision of facilities for recreation and any other object of general public utility. Indian public trusts are generally irrevocable. No national law governs public charitable trusts in India, although many states (particularly Maharashtra, Gujarat, Rajasthan, and Madhya Pradesh) have Public Trusts Acts that work in their areas only.

- **Societies:** Societies in India, are membership organizations that may be registered for charitable purposes. Societies are usually managed by a governing council or a managing committee. Societies are governed by the Societies Registration Act 1860, which has been adapted by various states. Unlike trusts, societies may be dissolved.

Non-profit Companies: A section 8 company (old section 25 company) is a company with limited liability that may be formed for "promoting commerce, art, science, religion, charity or any other useful object," provided that no profits, if any, or other income derived through promoting the company's objects may be distributed in any form to its members. (Source: *http://www.ngosindia.com/resources/ngo_registration1.php*)

1.3.9 The ten steps to Reduce NGO Registration Complexity

In order to reduce NGO registration complexity, Ryan Libre (2008), describes ten steps of how to successfully start an NGO:

Step 1: Testing the water

Join others who do similar work for a while before starting your own NGO. This will help you to gain experience and even copy some ideas from them.

Step 2: Start on the right foot

Becoming obsolete should be the fundamental goal of all NGOs. You must constantly strive to work yourself out of a job and aim at positive results.

Step 3: Clarify your goals and objectives

Set clear and achievable goals and objectives for yourself and the NGO.

Step 4: Make an action plan

A plan of action is your chance to make an NGO effective, address any potential negative impacts and make sure your NGO will attract donors and volunteers and finally serve the purpose.

Step 5: Develop/establish a website or social links

Be sure to make an online profile for your NGO where you can tap into a network of thousands of potential donors and volunteers. Establish a website for the donors to see your profile. Some hosting companies give free hosting to NGO sites. Establish or join social media to be connected all the time.

Step 6: Get in the know
Even if you grew up in the city where you want to start an NGO, you still need to research and make contacts. Good use of local and traditional knowledge can really make an NGO effective. Without local knowledge, you may do more harm than good.

Step 7: Assess your NGO's financial needs
Set up your budget and line it up with your sources of income. The balance between income and expenditure results in financial sustainability.

Step 8: Network, network, network
Make friendship with experienced people and organizations doing similar work so that you can learn from their successes and mistakes. Networking also helps you know when to team up and when to divide your efforts for maximum effectiveness.

Step 9: Find balance
Be realistic about how much time you want to give to your NGO. Taking on projects beyond your comfortable limits won't yield much benefit in the long run.

Step 10: Re-evaluate everything
Take a step back and look at what you have done and where it is all headed. Take joy in what you have accomplished, but also make sure your NGO is not becoming self-aggrandizing.

Libre, R. 2008 also commented that; "Any volunteer experience can be rewarding. Starting your own NGO can make you feel totally fulfilled. You will learn and grow as an individual and receive a profound sense of satisfaction not easily found in modern life" *(Libre, R. 2008 - How to start a successful NGO in 10 steps).*

The following phases are also important towards establishment, maintenance and sustaining the NGO.

Phase 1: The birth of an Idea

This is a stage where an idea is born by one individual and accepted by one or more individuals and later by a group of people. Since an NGO cannot be a one-person entity, then you need a group of people to support your idea and own it. The first group of people to support your idea are normally known as Founder members or Trustees.

Phase 2: Develop the NGO by-laws

As said above, the Constitution, Trust Deed, Memarts or the Memorandum and Articles of Association (as you name it) are not only used as requirements for registration purposes, but also contains rules, by laws and regulations that govern and regulate the functions of the NGO. Therefore, developing such documents needs great consideration to avoid misconception and conflict of powers.

Phase 3: Determine NGO Vision and Mission

Although sometimes this is found in the NGO constitution, Trust Deed, Memarts or the Articles of Memorandum, but it is an important part that will show where you want to reach (Vision) and the means to take you there (Mission).

Phase 4: Establish effective NGO's leadership

Establishment of Leadership procedures and leadership positions within the organization should be featured in the constitution for effective NGO functioning. This may include leadership organs (Meetings, Board of Directors, functional committees and other NGO organs) and NGO Leaders (including Members of the Board of Directors, Chairperson, Secretary, Treasurer and the Chief Executive Officer (CEO). However, it should be noted that NGO Managers are not Leaders, because functional officers who are sometimes referred to as NGO Managers are not included in NGO leaders.

Phase 5: Develop Fund-Raising and Resource Mobilization strategies

The proverb, *"You can't milk a starving cow"* applies when running a resourceless organization. Running an organization without resources of any kind, is like milking a starving cow.

Any NGO needs to be abundant with all required resources to be functional effectively and result oriented. Resources like human, financial and even materials are vital for any organization's existence. However, financial and resource sustainability is the result of sustainable funds and resource management. Your resources will be sustainable and value for money the way you will be cautious in their management. A strategy document on fund raising and resource mobilization, that will include management and sustainability, will ensure existence of the organization as well.

Once the NGO is established, the following procedures should be observed:

a) Establish Clear Vision

As earlier said, make sure the organization has a clear vision, a well-defined sense of purpose and an effective strategy for achieving this purpose. Visit your vision if it is included in the constitution. Make sure no one imposes ideas upon others and become monopoly.

b) Avoid "Founder Syndrome"

In some cases, Founder members tend to own the organization and always impose their ideas to be followed. Avoid this through involving all leaders, management team members and staff so that the organization is not dominated by one or few of the founder members who may take decisions on their personal interest and basis.

c) Ensure there are clear and logical structures

Good structures make the organization to function while organized. For effectiveness, one has to ensure the organization has clear and logical structures and administrative systems which are based on the main activities or functions of the organization. Make sure all leaders and staff know their roles and responsibilities. Concretely, the organization should have adequate financial management systems.

d) Ensure the organization remains financially secured

In order to maintain financial sustainability, one has to develop a financial sustainability strategy, financial regulations and financial accounting documents for internal effective controls. Don't let the donor influence the organization's financial policy as there are many other funding agencies, which might be interested with your financial policies if prepared adequately.

e) Avoid dominance

Make sure the organization is not controlled by one part or one person. All stakeholders should be involved i.e. organization members, the Board members, staff members, donors and the target group of the programme. Participatory approaches should be one of your organization's core values.

f) Develop staff development and motivation strategy

The organization staff should be motivated with good salary, allowances and benefits. Put in place the adequate staff career and development prospects. Ensure gender balance - place emphasis on equal participation of male and female in decision making as this will avoid jeopardizing one side of your team.

g) Avoid internal conflicts

Always manage, ignore and suppress internal conflicts within the organization. Maintain good relations between the professionals and volunteer staff, between headquarters and the field office, between the programme and support staff.

h) Maintain autonomy

The management style and the organizational culture should be appropriate and consistent to the organizational culture, such that they won't hinder the programmes and motivation of staff. Respect human rights principles in the programme and maintain autonomy in the programmes as this will bring about objectivity and fairness without undue influence on programmes and activities.

i) Establish the Board of Directors and give them autonomy to decision

The organization has to evaluate itself, learn from experience and adapt accordingly. It should be described as a "learning organization" and an "effective change agent" It should have capacity in terms of resources, specialist knowledge and organizational expertise to deliver effectively to the initiated programmes. Make sure the Board of Directors is functional and has full autonomy to decide on any matter concerning the growth of the organization. Ensure Project Management strategies and plans are in practice and functional.

j) Establish networking strategies with others

Try your best to make networking plans with other stakeholders are as useful as possible. Collaborate with other organizations with similar objectives to learn from each other in order to achieve common goals.

Using participatory approaches, all target groups and stakeholders should participate fully in planning, management, and evaluation of the organizational programmes. Provide sufficient resources to develop the organizational capacity of the local communities. Categorically, the programmes should respond to the expressed needs of the target group.

1.3.12 Derivation and Historical Development of CSOs/NGOs (The Case of Tanzania)

Private Voluntary Organizations are in the form of civic associations and religious organizations. They were introduced in Tanganyika by the colonial system, part of cultural transition. Notable among them were the Royal Society for the Prevention of Cruelty to Animals (TSPCA), Red Cross, Boy Scouts, etc. Soon after independence, some of them were transformed and/or affiliated into the ruling party fearing of their popularity in future, and instead Village Development Committees (VDCs) were formed to coordinate peoples' efforts at grassroot level. *(Muchunguzi D, (1993).*

The economic shocks of the 1970s and early 1980s made clear that Government alone cannot be expected to meet all the development needs of society. By 1984 the Government of Tanzania re-established cooperative societies, abolished District Councils and allowed people to form self-help organizations. *(Muchunguzi D, (1993).*

The political policy measures that followed after the crisis and the mult-partism movement of 1992 reinforced opportunities for CSOs and NGOs to flourish in the country. To date (2020) there are about 11,300 registered local and International NGOs operating in Tanzania alone.

The above historical background of NGOs, show how difficult it was to establish an NGO at that time. However, there are some countries which are still with such fears and mistrust among the NGOs. These countries, however, have to assess the contribution of Non-State Actors in the people's development and see how important are these development partners.

CHAPTER TWO

PROJECT DESIGN, IMPLEMENETATION AND MANAGEMENT

2.1 Definition of the term "Project"

A project is a provisional work or activity that perceives the beginning and partakes the finishing point while generating exceptional results. However, there are many definitions from different people and planners depending on the type of activity, the place and target group to benefit from that project.

Young, 2007, defines a project as "a collection of linked activities carried out in an organized manner with a clearly defined start point and finish point, to achieve some specific results that satisfy the needs of the organization's current business plans"

Lornmen D, 2016, defines a project as "a temporary endeavor with definite beginning and definite end undertaken to create a unique product or service"

Dr Gerald Brooks 2008, defines the project as "a temporary endeavour with a beginning and an end and it must be used to create a unique product, service or result". He further explains that, "A project is an activity to meet the creation of a unique product or service and thus activities that are undertaken to accomplish routine activities cannot be considered projects." *(Gerald Brooks 2008; -Project Management, Body of Knowledge).*

2.2 An overview of NGO Projects

NGO projects differ from other organizations' projects in their design. The NGO project is a unique venture and separate from normal organization work with a beginning and an end, conducted by people to meet established goals within parameters of cost, schedule and quality. It focuses to promote livelihood or give relief to a certain issue within the community. An NGO project is not-profit-oriented, it always has certain goals, a clear time frame and budget of which the result should benefit the entire community in which the project is implemented.

"NGOs worldwide perform a wide range of services aimed towards human wellbeing and social welfare. These organizations relentlessly work towards development and bringing a positive change in the society. NGOs may have different structures, activities and policies, but all NGOs are committed towards their cause and perform their functions to achieve their respective goals". *https://www3. fundsforngos.org/how-to-start-and-build-a-successful- ngo/1-2-functions-of-a-ngo/ (How to start and build a Successful NGO / 1.2 Functions of an NGO).*

2.3 NGO Roles in the Project Cycle

The World Bank (1995), developed a practical guide for their partners to use in their project operation cycles and implementation functions.

The following table provides a summary of the specific roles which NGOs can play at various stages of a project cycle. Each of the tasks described below requires specific skills and competencies (e.g. participatory methodologies, technical knowledge etc.) and individual NGOs must be selected accordingly. Levels of NGO experience vary significantly by country and sector, and therefore, the ability of NGOs to fulfill the tasks described below must be verified on a case-by-case basis.

Stage in Project Cycle	Potential NGO Involvement
Project Identification	• provide advice/information on local conditions • participate in environmental and social assessments • organize consultations with beneficiaries/ affected parties • transmit expressed needs/priorities of local communities to project staff • act as a source, model or sponsor of project ideas • implement pilot projects
Project Design	• consultant to the government, to local communities or to the Bank • assist in promoting a participatory approach to project design • channel information to local populations
Financing	• co-financier (in money or in kind) of a project component • source of funds for activities complementary to the proposed Bank-financed project

Implementation	• project contractor or manager (for delivery of services, training, construction, etc.) • promote community participation in project activities • financial intermediary role
	• supplier of technical knowledge to local beneficiaries • advisor to local communities on how to take advantage of project-financed goods or services • implementor of complementary activities • beneficiary of an NGO funding mechanism established by the project
Monitoring and Evaluation	• NGO contracted to monitor project progress or evaluate project results • facilitate participatory monitoring and evaluation • make use of independent/unsolicited monitoring and evaluation

Source: World Bank 1995, pp.29, *Working with NGOs - A Practical Guide to Operational Collaboration between the World Bank and Non-Governmental Organizations.*

2.4 Project Management

Project Management is a process used to control utilization of resources, supervision of activities and focusing on achieving the intended results as set in the objectives and measuring or assessing the outcome. This means, project managers have to manage resources, such as finance and human resources, supervise the work on the ground (activities), monitor and evaluate the progress and results.

Like the project itself, Project Management has been defined in many views.

Cook C.R. 2005, defines project management as a process, that; "project management is a series of steps undertaken to achieve a specific outcome" *Cook, C. R. (2005) - Just enough, Project Management.*

This means, one has to undertake many and different steps to make the project reach and show its intended results.

Young D. 2017, defines Project Management as "a dynamic process that utilizes the appropriate resources in a controlled and structured manner to achieve some clearly defined objectives identified as strategic needs" *Young D, 2017 - Project Management*

Project management is about knowing exactly what your goals are, how you're going to achieve them, what resources you'll need, and how long it will take you to reach that specific goal. In fact, project management's goal is to make sure that everyone involved in a project knows these and is aware of the purpose of the project.

The discipline itself is an organized manner of managing a project from its beginning to a defined ending. All projects need a structure. Hence, the complexity and length of the project are equivalent to a more advanced and detailed project plan.

The "project manager" is in-charge of the planning and execution of a project. He makes sure that everything is following the client's vision and quality standards. He will also be held accountable for the project's success or failure. *Alexandra Cote 2019, (Project Management Tools).*

2.4.1 The importance of Project Management

Without the concept of project management, a project's development would be chaotic. The discipline's main goal is to ensure that everyone involved in a project knows exactly what needs to be done, for how long they have to complete an activity, what resources are available and whom they should talk to in case they encounter a problem.

If everybody clearly knows what he has to do, there will be much higher chances of meeting the project's requirements. Also, mistakes that otherwise would require additional time to fix are eliminated from the start. These could lead you to lose important data and resources in the process. The main goal of project management is to ensure the final success of a project. A project is successful once all objectives have been followed on time and on budget and the client is pleased with the quality of the project.

There are many indicators that can demonstrate whether the project is on the right track or otherwise, collaboration and well-organized project strategies, implementors' commitment, availability of funds and resources and timely and effective correction of mistakes are some of indicators that can keep proper rolling of the project.

2.4.2 The Main Benefits of using Project Management principles in your daily work

i.   You can see what task you're assigned to and which resources should be used including budget and available tools.

ii.   By tracking your time, you can create timesheet reports, analyze them to find free time for additional tasks, establish the next steps of the project, or estimate deadlines for future projects.

iii.   The monitoring stage of project management allows you to identify errors and mistakes whenever they occur through a detailed look at what all employees are doing and which resources they are using.

iv.   Assigns a team members to solve problems using available resources within the available time frame.

v.   Different team members can be assigned to a project or task and collaborate in real time to successfully complete it.

vi.   Through project transparency, everyone in charge of a project will be able to see what the team is working on or bring their own contribution to the development of the project.

vii.   Project management allows you to gather information, log data that was not predictable on the go, and use it to make the right data-based decisions.

viii.   Allows your client to see everything that's going on with the project and suggest improvements whenever something is not going according to the project vision.

ix.   Project management might look complicated, but chances are you've already been involved in a process such as this one. So, next time you're planning your friend's birthday, know that you're actually working on a project and you are your own project manager. *(Alexandra Cote 2019, Project Management Tools)*

2.5 The Project Cycle (Steps of Project Management)

The project management process as an activity, has different steps and levels known as "the project cycle" which include

Project initiation, Project planning and design, Project implementation or management, results assessment or monitoring and closure.

Figure No. 1: Project cycle

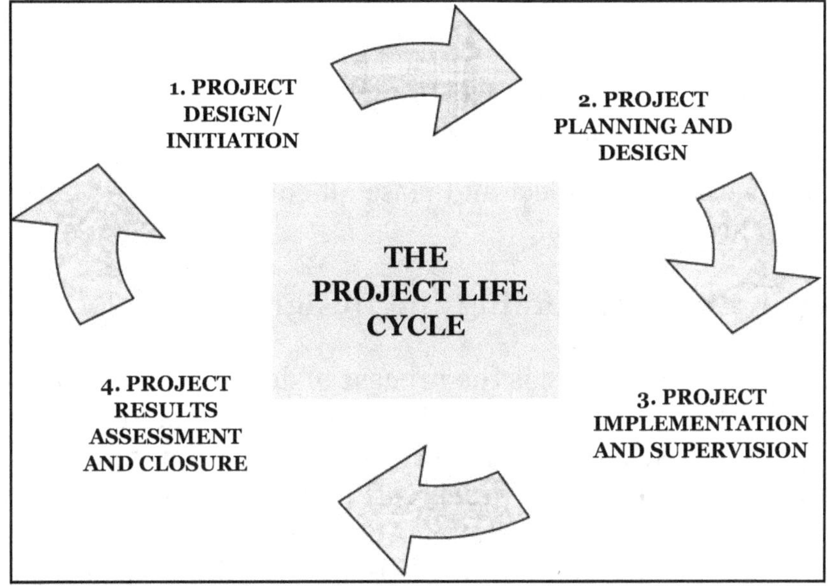

Step 1. Project Design/Initiation

Project Design or Initiation is the initial step in the process. It is a stage at which the basic project structure, the main external factors and some of the main elements of the monitoring system are identified. This may include an idea, commencement of the project, selection of key project workers such as the project manager and sometimes, developing a project concept. Other consideration at this stage include:

- In order to determine the project goals, first you have to discover what are the community needs, what is the existing situation and which group is most affected.

- Elaborating a plan that will tell you what needs to be done, by whom, how much it will cost, and when the project should be delivered. Sometimes, projects can follow four phases if project execution is done together with monitoring activities.

- Starting working.

- Checking if work goes according to the initial plan, identify problems, and make adjustments.

- Delivering the project and close all contracts once you get the client's approval.

Step 2. Project Planning and Design

Since project planning is the process of developing a detailed plan for the project that includes the task list, resources assignment, schedule, budget, communication plan, risk plan and change control process; this step, therefore, focuses on planning the costs, time and other resources needed for the project implementation. It is at this time the project document can be developed.

Step 3: Project Implementation and Supervision

This step is sometimes known as the Project Execution and Control. It is the time when technical work and expertise are needed. All planned activities have to be executed under this phase or step. In many cases, project implementation goes simultaneously with monitoring activities which are done to assess the Project Progression and Performance. Sometimes, even if the project will come to an end, the key staff such as the project manager may remain at work as there might still be some tasks to accomplish.

Step 4: Project Assessment, Evaluation and Closure

This is a stage where the project is accomplished and evaluation of its results done. In most cases, if the achievement is reached and the objectives realized, all resources will have been used out, work contracts with project staff will be terminated, come to an end or put in place other contracts of staff if there may be extension of the project or a new phase of the project has been determined.

CHAPTER THREE

FUND RAISING AND RESOURCE MOBILIZATION

3.1 Fund Raising and/or Resource Mobilization is a blood of any organization

This is because, NGOs merely rely on funding, whether from donors, private funding agencies and well-wishers or from the public institutions. NGOs, like any other entity, needs income in terms of human, financial and material resources in order to achieve their vision, mission and objectives. They need what is known as "the 4M" (Manpower, Money, Materials, and Machines), the resources which are prerequisite for any organization's development and are militarized through various strategies and approaches including fundraising and resource mobilization.

3.2 Definition of Fund Raising

Fund raising is a systematic approach of mobilizing resources from supporters to facilitate achievement of the organizational goals. It includes plans, activities, processes or events of raising funds through voluntary contributions of money or other resources by requesting donations from individuals, business, charitable foundations or government agencies. Fund raising is, therefore, mobilizing financial and non-financial resources necessary for the work of an organization and its plans.

35

Nevertheless, Fund Raising is a positive, but, very hard work, time consuming and tasking for most of organizations, but it is, however, practically straightforward if all procedures are followed keenly. These procedures, therefore, calls for patience, proper planning and comprehension. Some people think fundraising is begging, <u>NO</u>, Fundraising is <u>NOT</u> begging, it is mobilizing resources for the people or organizations to help other people. A bigger funding agency will mobilize resources from other sources and give them to another organization, that organization may give these resources to another organization as well or direct to the needy people or communities.

Fund raising is a very hard work despite being straight forward conceptually as it takes time, patience and planning. It is a task of asking for a specific amount of money and other specific resources from others. It is not just guessing what could be the need, but the precise need.

For effective fundraising exercise, an organization should have the following key elements:

i.   Knowing the current need of an organization and the community it strives to serve.

ii.   Knowing the sources of income, it gets and/or can get through maintaining a directory of funders and other sources of income.

iii. Having regular communications and maintain healthy relationships with the potential funders and other organizations who can provide money or other resources to the organization.

iv.   Formulating clear fund-raising objectives and strategies

v.   Preparing, archiving and selling concepts and proposals that attract funding sources and telling stories (Problem statements) that inspire people to give.

3.3 What is Resource Mobilization?

Resource Mobilization (RM) is a systematic approach and process of mobilizing different types of support from different sources for an organization, the community or the Government to facilitate achievement of its goals.

Resource mobilization is not far from Fund Raising, because they are all the processes of actions executed to collect resources such as financial, human and material resources to promote a mission of an organization. These kinds of actions; when successful, maintains the sustainability of an organization or institution. The main aim of RM is to reduce the organization's dependence on donor support and maintain resource equity and sustainability.

3.4 Planning for a Fund-Raising and Resource Mobilization Activity

In planning for a fund-raising activity, many steps are needed to accomplish the plan; however, six of them are imperative to develop a successful/practicable Fund-Raising and Resource Mobilization Strategy.

Step 1: Establishing a fundraising goal

Before a fundraising activity is performed, a goal of your fundraising plan is to be established. This will include the amount of money needed to be raised and what the money will be used for. In case the fundraising activity has many goals, each goal should have its fund-raising plan. However, the fundraising goal can't be developed by one individual; but needs to involve all key players within an organization such as the Members of Board of Director, Management team, some organization staff and for participatory purposes, involvement of other stakeholders from the community is of vital importance.

Step 2: Develop a strategic fundraising plan/strategy

Developing a fundraising plan is not just to put down a list of needed resources and their cost, but, includes also developing a plan that is written strategically and states how much money is needed to be raised, what are the sources, how it will be used and which strategies/methods should be used to reach the intended goal.

Step 3: Estimate the cost of your fundraising plan

The budget of the fundraising plan does not mean the cost for the programme you want to implement. It is just the cost for the fund-raising activity. Make sure you include costs such as advertisement costs for a fund-raising activity, venue costs if needed for special events, costs for consultants, staff and volunteers who will perform the fundraising activity, postage, secretarial services and stationery costs. Make sure the budget is cost-effective and make the fund-raising cost as small as possible as compared to the intended project budget. Normally, some funding raising experts estimate not more that 15% of the intended project budget and facilitates the cost for the fundraising activity to be recovered during the event.

Step 4: Set a time frame for your fundraising plan

It is good to develop an action plan that will include a time frame for each activity, identify who will be responsible for each of those activities and specify who will be the leader of the whole process. Setting time frame will help the implementers to follow the calendar without interrupting each other as it will show the project start up, its consequent implementation and accomplishment within the specified time. The time line can change as the time pass and basing on the current situation and environment within and without the organization.

Step 5: Search for funding sources

Many people just jump to the fundraising activity without collecting information about the funding sources. This is not right, whatever the fundraising activity is, you need to identify who is the anticipated and/or potential funding source. If it is a donor, identify to whom you will send your project proposal, if it is an event-based fundraising, identify who are to be invited to attend the event and their capacity to contribute, if your target are individuals, find out whom you will visit or send your fundraising request; et cetra. Ensure current sources are not leveraged so that they can produce more income to your organization.

Step 6: Develop and implement your fundraising evaluation plan

Evaluation is an important factor in the life of any project/plan as among others, it identifies what components of an initiative or plan do not work well and why, as well as identifying areas that need improvement in order to provide the best results.

It is good to have an evaluation plan of your fundraising strategy to evaluate the outcome at every certain period, say after three, six or twelve months. Include in the evaluation plan, the evaluation approach or methodology, time frame, means of verification of your results and if possible, the cost of your evaluation activity. If your fund-raising activity is a multi-year plan, then plan annual evaluation instead of monthly or quarterly evaluation.

Additionally, the Fundraising strategy should also consider the following:

i.   Clear understanding

The fundraiser should clearly understand the vision and mission of the organization and be able to clearly explain this to the donor and the beneficiary community.

ii.   Educate the potential donor

Inform the donor about the organization, needed resources and what would be the impact of the proposed project on the beneficiary community.

iii. Maintain relationships

Establish and maintain good relations with all organizations, public sectors and target groups.

3.5 Types of Fund-Raising Strategies and Methods (Source of Funds)

There are many ways in which an organization can fundraise or mobilize resources for her sustainability. Most of these strategies and methods are possible at an organization level but also at the community level, especially when the latter is involved in what is known as Participatory Resource Mobilization (PRM). Some common strategies include:

i. Self-Contribution (Community Contribution): This includes membership fees and constitutional subscription from members. (This is most common in Tanzania).

ii.   Project proposal writing to Donors (selling concepts and proposals that attract funding).

iii.   Event-based fundraising (Organizing fundraising events), such as dinners, community festivals, sports activities, auction and sale of products and local philanthropy activities.

iii.   Online project concept advertisement (Advertising the project concept on the internet, Websites, media and other publications to enrich resource providers).

iv.   Face to face contacts or electronic communication to the donors and other funding agents and telling stories that inspire them to give.

v.   Lobbying for funding and sometimes advocacy strategies (To advocate on behalf of the target group i.e. communities).

vi.   Income Generation Activities (IGAs) or investments (Establishment of income generation activities within an organization such as Small business and permanent investments).

Among all those above, in this Chapter, we shall dwell in project proposal writing which is more common for most development practitioners especially the NGO sector and appropriate for most of funding sources.

CHAPTER FOUR

WRITING A PROJECT PROPOSAL

4.1 The Project Proposal

Writing a project proposal is the most useful strategy as it gives clear vision of the project concept. A project proposal is, therefore, an important tool for organizing time and mobilizing resources to complete a project, which fully realizes the organization's objectives. On the research context, a project proposal is very useful in structuring research ideas on how the research will be carried out, the methodologies, costs involved, recommendations and conclusions.

Convincingly; the project proposal is a professional scientific fund-raising tool in the development arena. Funding agents normally gain knowledge of the project concept theoretically before they decide to approve the request. This means, project proposals should be a convincing tool to the funding agents that the project is viable and can reduce the identified issue in the community. Practically, a project proposal does not serve just for seeking grants from donors. It can also be used as a business plan in the business arena, it is as well a working tool which can be used by organization staff and experts as a reference document while executing their projects, even if they are self-funded.

4.2 Project Proposal Formats

Project proposals have a variety of formats depending on the requirements by the funding source. Project Proposals written and submitted to the big foundations, international NGOs (INGOs), UN systems and those written for state donations will obviously differ in their final form. Foundations and INGOs usually require a brief letter while federal agencies usually require the applicant to complete an extensive array of forms and possibly attach narrative documents. Nevertheless, the contents of a project proposal will depend on many circumstances like the type of a funding source/donor. Many donors have their own formats in which they assess the proposal basing on such formats.

However, there should be a standard format that is a base for all donors and funding agents to follow. The following standard project proposal format is a basic planning format for all proposals. Thinking through various sections will enable the applicant to draw from the content virtually all that either a private or public funding source will ask from you. Additionally, various components in this format will enable the applicant to develop a logical way to approach the organization's plans and programs and hopefully this planning will make the programs more effective.

The standard project proposal format has 10 (standard) sections that can be changed in the logical flow, but the concept remains the same.

4.3 Types of Project Proposals

There are many types of project proposal used to solicit funds from funding agencies, therefore before you start writing, you should know what kind of project proposal you want to write before you waste your time on unwanted basics and leave the important ones. It is, therefore, important to involve the whole management team in deciding which type of project proposal is required.

However, the most common types of proposals are six as provided below:

4.3.1 Advertised proposals

An advertised proposal, is a project proposal which is formerly solicited by the funding agency through advertisements known as "Call for proposals" or "Expression of Interest". In most cases, such call for proposals are accompanied with forms or proposal templates to be filled by the applicant. Also, this type of a proposal is good and easy because the templates tell what is needed to be written in each specific section. Call for proposal templates are always concise and clear such that needs carefulness while filling the forms, because sometimes the words and/or characters in each section are limited. For such proposals a structured approach is needed because the contents are clear and no one can insert his/her own even if they look challenging or otherwise.

4.3.2 Informally solicited proposal

Informally solicited project proposals are the same as advertised or formerly solicited proposals, but they differ in their information and contents. Sometimes, the informally solicited proposal, although it gives information on what is needed to be written as a proposal, but are not accompanied with templates, which cause difficulties in preparing them.

Mulholland B. 2017, insists that; "It's pretty much just a lack of detail that separates formal from informal – formal proposal requests have set details, goals, deliverables, and potentially even methods, while informal ones could be based on a conversation. If you've been asked for a proposal but haven't been given any specifics, it's an informally solicited one" *Mulholland B, 2017-Six Types of Project Proposal That Get Approved...*

Mulholland B. 2017, further insists that; "the approach for this isn't too different from a formally solicited one, but you'll have to put in some extra legwork in defining details like the objectives and method, and in assessing how viable the whole thing is."

When preparing a proposal which is informally solicited, you can use a template from a formally solicited project proposal that will help you with contents.

4.3.3 Unsolicited project proposal

Unsolicited project proposals are the proposals which are prepared by the applicant(s) without advertisement or no any agency has asked for them. This type is common because most of development practitioners prepares a project document and search for donors where they can sell them. When writing such a proposal, then a standard format of proposal writing is applied. Some consultants do prepare such project proposals and keep them in their document banks (hardcopy or soft copy) waiting to sell them to the funding agency. However, you can use a template from the call for proposal and use the format to accomplish your document.

Mulholland B, 2017, further maintain on this, that; "Arguably, these are the hardest proposals to write, as you'll have to be extra persuasive (nobody asked for the proposal so they'll need extra nudging). This means gathering more evidence than usual to prove the proposal's worth and taking extra care when writing to make sure that it's convincing" *Mulholland B, 2017- 6 Types of Project Proposals That Get Approved...*

4.3.4 Extension project proposals

This type of a proposal is written when the project is being extended or changing from one project phase to another. They are sometimes called Continuation project proposals and are very easy to write because the concept and its components do not change, they remain the same. Also, because such projects are already approved, you don't need much efforts to think on what to write. You may need to work on just the Budget, extend or change the project area and or embark on new project approaches.

4.3.5 Regeneration project proposals

The regeneration project proposal is also termed by Mulholland B. 2017, as the "renewal project proposal". It is not far different from the continuation project proposal because it is written if the applicant organization wants to continue with the same funding source. The difference is, with the continuation project proposal, the project is the same while the renewal proposal the project and even the concept can change. Like how it is a continuation proposal, grant seekers by this proposal do not need much information to the funders because they will have known each other and at this time, the funder might have been gratified to continue with the working relationship. While writing both the Continuation and the renewal or regeneration proposal, efforts must be examining the outcome of the former/ending project and document the lesson learned and build on their success.

4.3.6 Supplemental project request

A supplemental project proposal is not as big as a conventional project proposal, it is written when extra funds are needed beyond the original budget to accomplish the project activities. This can be in a form of a letter of one or two pages explaining required additional funding for the project. The grant seeker needs to justify why extra funding is needed. Reasons can be the exchange rate fluctuation, changes in the country economy, increased project scope to reach wider areas and having new vision that might change original goals, unforeseen hardships and challenges while implementing the current project and even the need for the project outcome realization. In any reason, the applicant should inform the funder why such problems were not seen during project design and preparation and then emphasis reiterating on the benefits that the supplement funding will bring in.

4.4 Planning for Project Proposal Writing

Before you write a project proposal, various scenarios have to be observed and ensured that will shape a way to a project proposal that can be viable and attainable in the face of a funding agent.

The following steps are very important before the project proposal is written:

Step 1: Apprehend the project idea

The project idea is a step where the grant seeker must observe. It is when the development practitioner identifies a development issue(s) within the community. The idea cannot just be conceived from nowhere; it is a result of an observed problem within the concerned community. It might be from the research, government reports or observing existing problems that the community face at a specific time like the disease outbreak and disasters.

Step 2: Examine your organization's mission and goals

Once you have identified a specific development problem within the community, the second step is to revisit your originations vision and mission to confirm that the problem you want your project to solve is within the organization's Mission and Goals. It is always ambiguous if your organization embark on a programme which is not in your set of goals and objectives. That is why most funders ask for the Vison, Mission, Goals/purpose and objectives of your organization. If they find that the project you are proposing is not stipulated in your constitution for example, the funder will not give out funds. They tend to name such proposals a "shopping document" meaning that, you prepared it for the aim of shopping donor funds. However, strategic plan, fund raising policy and a long-term plan of an organization, are some documents that can be revisited to ensure the appropriateness of the project you want to present to the donor.

Step 3: Examine your Working Environment

Grant seekers have to analyze their working environment they are working in. This can be done through assessing the Political, Economic, Social and Technological (PEST) factors that might have an impact on the project, the organization, your fundraising efforts and its implementation strategies. Also, you can use **SWOT** analysis tool to scan your organization's Strength, Weakness, Opportunities and Threats that can impact the project outcome.

However, **SWOT:** is an acronym of **Strength, Weakness, Opportunities and Threats**. SWOT analysis is very indispensable especially when formulating fundamental management programmes particularly in planning and visioning. SWOT analysis is an analytical tool used to identify and categorize significant internal (Strength and Weakness) and external (Opportunities and Threats) factors faced by an organization. When SWOT analysis is carried out, some issues that might be addressed may among others include; an extent to which the NGO's work is known and regarded or appreciated such as having a good number of quality supporters, committed workers, Good will among the staff, supporters and the Government (Strength). Also, to assess the Weakness on an organization, screening should examine if the organization has no or inadequate supporters, inadequate resources including human resources, lack of unity and teamwork among the organization and ineffective workers' performance. Concerning the opportunities of an organization, issues like; Good will by the supporters and the government, community participation, skilled staff in fund raising and NGO management and having good working environment. Threats which might be out of the organization's capacity may include; poor relationship with the government, Lack of skilled staff with fund raising capacities, competition in service delivery within the same area, Donors requirements etc.

Eyre 1993; defined the issues involved in **SWOT** acronym as summarized hereunder by (David Lornmen, 2016):

1. **Strength:** These are aspects of an organization such as exceptional goodwill, brand loyalty, highly trained efficient staff, enormous financial resources and a strong marketing team. Strength are the bedrock on which an organization can build success. Usually the elements are internal factors over which the organization has ample influence.

2. **Weakness:** These represent the retarding influence on the success and growth of the organization. They may be

obsolescent equipment, no provision for management succession, inadequate research and development facilities, lack of new products to succeed those declining etc. The organization must undertake a critical soul, searching honest investigation to objectively establish its weakness profile; then it must proceed to undertake programmes or steps to remedy the situation. Weakness are too largely internal factors and the organization has a large measure of control over them.

3. **Opportunities:** Unlike strength and weakness which emanate chiefly from inside the organization, opportunities are usually external. Examples include new markets openings in which the organization has advantage over competition, opportunity to take over company that would considerably improve market position, the appointment of a close associate to high government position that can facilitate huge contracts, etc.

4. **Threats:** These are situations which present disadvantageous repercussions on the organization. Management complacency, a serious internal threat, is a classic example. Poor financial management and low staff morale are others in the category. Rapid changes in technology and government policies, political instability and business cycles are examples of external threats to the operation of an organization. Source on (SWOT): (*David Lornmen, 2016, - Selected Top Secrets of Success for Managers and Leaders*).

Step 4: Identify and understand your funding source

Many grant seekers fail to observe this step. They just read thoroughly in the call for proposal or having just the address of the funding agent. This might cause wastage of time and resources because each funding source has their own funding criterion, guidelines and main focus of the fund. It is important, therefore, to take time gratifying oneself on; what does the funder prioritize and what they are not ready to fund, which format of the proposal they want, what is the focus and which is the budget ceiling. You have to understand also, which type of projects they fund and which not, the areas/location they work in and time frame of the funding. This stage is also known as "the funding analysis." So, the first thing needed to do when planning a project proposal is to outline your anticipated funding source. This stage also helps you to know the problem you want to solve in the funders' criterion and they can regard your project as a relief to that problem. Also, successful funding often depends on the building long term relationship between the partners. The three or four funders on your list may have years of experience in your field of activity, or they may be interested in building experience in your field and in your country or region. "Remember, this is the driving force behind getting your approval. Your audience (funding source) provides the context, but the problem you're solving gives purpose – a reason to care about (and approve) the entire project in the first place" (*Mulholland_B, 2017- 6 Types of Project Proposals That Get Approved...*)

Step 5: Study the magnitude of the problem

You can't look for solution of any problem if you don't know its scope. This can be done by reviewing the past studies on that problem and what is the recommended solution by the researchers. Also, the government offices might have reports on how they know this problem and what are the government guidelines on how to solve it.

If the resources allow, it is very important to conduct what is known as baseline survey to assess the greatness of the problem and thereafter implement what you are sure with. This kind of survey will also give out a benchmark of your project that will help you to gauge the baseline data and the outcome during project evaluation. If your organization has good knowledge on the problem, then use that data to explain how big is the problem and its possible solution. The information here must be data based and evidently grounded. This step needs a teamwork as it requires much input to convince a funder that the project is viable for funding, because if the funding source themselves are familiar with the specified problem, then they will put much emphasis to examine if the proposed methodology you want to use is appropriate to solve it.

Step 6: Identify/appoint a technical team to write a project proposal

Not all development practitioners or organization staff have skills to write a project proposal. Some proposals need technical inputs which the organization staff don't or few have. It is, therefore, important to assess your team for technical input to each specific project proposal. If the team members lack expertise on specific proposals, then an external expert or consultant might be needed to join the team. However, it is not advisable to just engage the consultant to write a proposal without involvement of your staff members as the latter are more conversant with the organization's state of affairs and sometimes with good knowledge of the problem your proposal wants to solve than the consultant. The proposal prepared in a team works better than that of one minded idea.

Step 7: Forecast the outcome of your proposal

My Instructor, Dr. Jim Campbell, at the Institute of Cultural Affairs, (ICS, Belgium) told me in 1994 that "Once you prepare a feasible project proposal that you are satisfied with its contents, you ought to forecast its approval and therefore you can open a champagne to celebrate beforehand". This might be true, because when you feel there are some uncertainties and questions left in your proposal, the funding source will have more of them and that will be the end of your project approval. Questions like, "why this project is the best solution to solve the identified problem?", "is the budget value for money?" are the proposed methods to implement the project appropriate to achieve the intended goal? should be asked by the team members and replied in the project proposal itself. With this in mind, construction of the problem statement and developing the logical framework matrix will be easy for the team. Remember, successful funding is the result of a good project proposal and that begins within your organization.

CHAPTER FIVE

ELEMENTS OF A PROJECT PROPOSAL

Now you have done a ground work to establish and put a base for your project document, then you need to have the required tools, material and equipment in place, ready for proposal writing. The following are key elements or steps known as sections; that should be followed when writing a standard project proposal.

5.1 Key Elements/Sections of a Standard Project Proposal

a) Project summary

b) Introduction/Background Information

c) Project Rationale

d) Problem Statement

e) Project Goals and Objectives

f) Strategies and Activities

g) Project Results

h) Project Benefits

i) Beneficiaries

j) Sustainability plan/Future Funding

k) Project Monitoring and Evaluation mechanisms

    i.   Workplan or action plan

    ii. Logical Framework Analysis

    iii. Monitoring schedule/plan

l) Project Budget and estimates

m) Annexes and appendices

    i.   Stakeholder Mapping Analysis matrix

    ii. Photographs, Reports, Testimonies etc.

5.2 Guidelines for Writing a Generic/Standard Proposal

Table No: 6: Contents for the standard Project Proposal

Part One	**PROPOSAL SUMMARY** Clear, concise, specific summary of proposal	**CONTENTS** Same contents but summarized project proposal • Explain Who you are • The scope of project • Project Cost
Purpose Content		
Section 1 Purpose Content	**INTRODUCTION** Organizational Credibility • History of an organization • Significant accomplishments • Organizational goals and uniqueness • Support from other organizations	**INFORMATION ABOUT ORGANIZATION** • Organizational Purpose • Evolution • Legal status • Affiliation (if any) • Organizational Structure • Board and Staffing pattern • Board and Staff Size • Current Programmes and Projects • Experience with similar activities

Section 2 Purpose Content	**PROBLEM STATEMENT/ RATIONALE** Documenting the problem • Document existence of a problem with key statistics • Make connection between your organization and problem • Define a problem as you intend to work on	**BACKGROUND TO THE PROPOSED PROJECT** Rational for the Particular project • Project context – central development which make this project necessary and setting which effects the problems can cause. • Beneficiaries: those affected or may be affected by the problem. • Needs assessment process.
Section 3 Purpose Content	**PROJECT OBJECTIVES** Measurable results • Concrete measurable objectives • What are results of the proposed activities? • What are differences that will come as results of the problem	**PROJECT DESCRIPTION** What will be the accomplishment and how it will be done? • Programme Objectives, specific impacts, stated quantitatively whenever possible and time frame
Section 4 Purpose Content	**ACTIVITIES/ METHODS** Actions to be executed to ensure the project bring about results/changes • Activities to be implemented • Analyzing why these methods and activities	**WORK PLAN** What will be done and who will do what • Sequential work plan components which includes methods/activities. • Project management and administration – how does it fit into organization; how do beneficiaries participate

Section 5 Purpose Content	**EVALUATION** Interpretation of results • Assess how effective was the programme tool for adjustment • What are beginning/ baseline indicators • What are the expected ending indicators? • What change to be brought about by the results from beginning indicators to ending indicators	**SELF MONITORING AND EVALUATION** Participatory Monitoring and evaluation • How you will systematically monitor progress management for objectives • What lesson learnt from the results and how this lesson will be replicated. • What are future prospects from the results (recommendations)
Section 6 Purpose Content	**FUTURE FUNDING** How will the project continue when grant runs out? • Prior project ownership by the beneficiaries and concerned stakeholders. • Commitment from the government and local communities. • Establishment of Income Generation systems from within an organization.	**PROJECT SUSTAINABILITY PLAN** What are available resources to make the project continue to exist. • Participatory mechanism for ensuring ownership • Who will carry out activities after the end of project? • Who, where, and how is accountability of the set mechanism?

	BUDGET Estimates needed resources to accomplish the project activities • Operational budget (costs for day-to-day running of an organization) • Capital budget (costs for procurement of assets and liabilities)	**FINANCIAL ESTIMATES** The cost of defined project activities (i.e. all items must be traceable to project activities description. (budget is the cost of activities) • Summarizes the total cost for human, financial and material resources needed for the project. • Indicates clearly the contribution from both, the donor and the recipient organization.
Section 7 Purpose Content		
Part 2	**SUPPORTING DOCUMENTS**	**ANNEXES (APPENDIXES)**

(Source: Grantsmanship Center, through ICA Belgium, ITPDP-1994 Training manual)

5.3 Logical Flow of a Generic/Standard Project Proposal

i. The Cover Page

The cover page is as well important as a covering letter. The cover page should contain the following:

(i) The organization Name

(ii) The origination Logo (if any)

(iii) The project Title (The title should be precise and informative on the project itself)

(iv) The Contact information including contacts i.e. Telephone, Fax, E-mail, Postal address, physical location and the contact person (Name and Title).

ii). The Summary

The project summary is the whole project document that describes all parts of a project proposal in a short form. It is a very important part of the project proposal because it is the first thing that a funding source will read. Sometimes, they may make decision basing on the quality of the summary page. The project summary should therefore be clear, brief and precise. It should show the image of your organization, as who you are, the viability of your project and the expected costs to be expended during the project implementation.

Most of the funding agents such as donors and international organizations, usually screen project documents before they decide whether to fund the project or not. They briefly examine each proposal to see if they are consistent with their priorities, and if it is from an organization eligible to apply for their funds. The following step, these screeners, always put up their own summaries that will be used to review the project applications in the third step of the process. It is, therefore, very important to spend much time on drawing your own summary that will attract the funding source and can be used to assess your application than to just hope that the reviewer sees the importance of your programme in his brief initial look at your proposal. The project summary is written after the proposal has been complete but should appear on the first part of the project document.

Section 1: Introduction

This is the section of a proposal where the applicant tells the background of the organization. Many proposals tell title or nothing about the applicant organization and speak only about the project or program to be conducted. More often than not, proposals are funded on the basis of the reputation or "connections" of the applicant organization or its key personnel rather than on basis of the program's content alone. The introduction is the section in which you build your credibility as an organization which should be supported.

However, Credibility is a status which gives an organization integrity in the eyes of a funding source, and this depends on the type of a funding source. For instance; a traditional or rather conservative funding source will be more responsive to persons or prominence on your Board of Directors, how long you have been in existence, how many other funding sources have been supporting you and other similar characteristics of your organization. An "avant-garde" (unconventional) funding source might be more interested in a Board of "community persons" rather than of prominent citizens or in organizations that are new rather than those long established etc.

Potential funding sources should be selected because of their possible interest in your type of organization or your type of program. You can use the introduction to reinforce the connection you see between your interests and those of the funding source. Additionally, successful funding usually commences at a top management to top management level, from director to director or board members to board members. Usually funding sources do not simply support the words and text of written project proposals; they fund the people who can be answerable and can execute these proposals effectively, merely basing on their integrity, trustworthy and their historical background. Therefore, it is important to include in the introduction section, the profile of the top leadership of an organization and qualifications of the key staff.

Some of the things you can say about your organization in an introduction section.

- How you got started - the historical background of your organization.

- How long you have been around - the duration which your organization has been operating in the riparian community

- Anything unique about the way you got started, or the fact you were the first thus-s-and-so organization in the country, etc.

- Some of your most significant accomplishments as an organization or, if you are a new organization, some of the significant accomplishments of your Board or staff in their previous roles.

- Your organization goals – why you were started.

- What support you have received from other organizations and prominent individuals (accompanied by some letter of endorsement which can be in an appendix)

- What achievements has your organization achieved, awards, letter of appreciation from development partners, the government and other renowned authorities.

It is however, strongly advised that, a "credibility file" be established, which can be used as a basis for introductory section and can support your project application for future proposals you write. Supporting documents such as copies of newspaper articles, recommendations from authorities in the government and partners, certificates of merit and awards. This is because, even if the proposal writer may be new to the organization, but there is a reference where he/she can find information. Remember, the credibility you establish in your introduction section may be more important than the rest of your project proposal. Build it, but here, as in all of your proposal, be as brief and specific as you can. Avoid jargons and keep it simple.

Section 2: Project Rationale and Problem Statement

a) The Project Rationale

The project rationale is a section where one has to justify why this project is needed and what are the evidence-based issues the project wants to address. It is a clarification that provides a comprehensive description of why the project is required at this time. The project rationale is sometimes known as the "project background" which forms the foundation of a proposal.   "It helps to give a valid reason for the project execution in the mentioned place. A donor will be familiar with the project area if the correct and reliable data are collected." *http:// proposalsforngos.com/category/sample-proposals/*

However, some people confuse the "project rationale" with the "problem statement". These are not the same, because, while the rationale is the justification on the importance of the project to address the identified problem(s) with the sought funding, the problem statement clarifies issues that the riparian community is facing and their extent. The rationale is a section in which you need to convince the funding source that the proposed project is needed at this time and not later and that your organization knows the scale of a problem that the project aims to address. You need also to give evidences of the problem greatness like the previous studies/researches, documents experience reports and documents from authorities such as government guidelines. This part of a project proposal is important because it demonstrates to your funding source that you know what you are applying for and that your project is strategic and viable. "An important part of this section should be a short description of your organization. After the donor has read and understood the problems and issues of the area, it may want to know why your organization is the best choice for addressing them. In the description of the organization, make sure you refer to your previous projects implemented similarly and/ or you can highlight the innovative idea you have for this project" _https://www.fundsforngos. org/free-resources-for-ngos/project-rationale-proposal/_

b) Problem Statement

A problem statement is a strong summarized clarification of issue(s) or problem(s) found in the community, which should be addressed by the project you are proposing.

In the introduction section you have been told on the credibility of your organization, you have explained who you are and justified the necessity for the funding source to see that you are eligible for funding. In this section, the funding source should now know the field in which you want to work in and the specific problem or problems that you want to solve through the project you are proposing. In this section, you need to make the funding source conscious of the problems affecting the community you want to serve.

Christ, 2009, wrote in his blog that; using the 5W's - Who, What, Where, When and Why - is a great tool that helps to get pertinent information out for discussion. The 5Ws will, therefore, examine what is happening within the concerned community and how the issues will be addressed by this project. _(Chris's blog, 2009, how to write a problem statement). http://www. ceptara.com/blog/how-to-write-problem-statement_

The 5 "Ws" (What, Who, When, Where, Why)

1. **What** – Examines; What is the current problem in the community you serve? What are the limitations of the problem? Is it within the organization? Is it geographic-within the location you are working in? What is the impact of the issue – short term or long term? - What impact is the issue causing? - What will

happen when it is fixed? - What would happen if this problem is not solved?

2. Who – Examines; Who is affected by the problem(s) or issue(s)? Are they specific groups, the whole community around, customers in a case of business?

3. When – Examines; When does the issue happen? Always, periodically or in some cases? When does it need to be fixed - immediately, later, need more time?

4. Where – Examines; Where is the issue happening? Only in this community or beyond? In certain locations, the whole Nation, in the region?

5. Why – Examines; Why is it significant that we fix the problem now? – Can't it wait? Why are these resources needed at this time?

When all answers are responded to, then you have a base to describe each issue specifically and that will pave your way to construct a problem statement. Again, **Chris 2009,** suggests that "Your problem statement should be solvable. That is, it should take a reasonable amount of time to formulate, try and deploy a potential solution. Remember, "a problem well stated is half solved", the better the clarity around what the team is attempting to fix, the more efficient they'll be in solving the problem, the solution will better 'fix' the issues and the team can get back to executing the business versus fixing it.". *(Chris's blog,2009, how to write a problem statement). http://www. ceptara.com/blog/how-to-write-problem-statement*

There are some pitfalls which many organizations face when they try to define problems. Sometimes they will state an immediate problem without dwelling to the big picture that exists in the community. They, however, do not narrow down to a specific problem that face the entire community, they sometimes hook their ideas to a specific group within the community.

In order to define a solvable problem, one has to draw a picture of a needy community in all its dimensions to make the funding source convinced that there are really problems there, and if not solved, the concerned community is in danger. Narrow down your definition of the problems you want to deal with to something you can hope to accomplish within a reasonable amount of time and with reasonable additional resources.

Again, clearly demonstrate your knowledge of the problem to convince your funding source that you really know that a problem exists, not just from researches and reports, but you have evidences that show your acquaintance on the magnitude of this problem.

Conclusively, don't fill your proposal with tables, charts and graphs as this may probably turn off the reader, if needed, save them for an appendix but pull out the key figures and statistics for your problem statement. Present a workable problem with clear relevant support. Make logical connection between your organization's background and the problems and needs which you propose to work. As mentioned above, support the existence of the problem by evidence. You may also get advice from groups in your community concerned about the problem, from prospective clients, and from other organizations working in your community as well as from other professionals in the field. Make sure that what you want to do is workable – that it can be done within a reasonable time, by you and with a reasonable amount of money.

Section 3: The Project Goal and Objectives

The first step towards developing a project proposal is to set the project goal that often lays the foundation for the project. The goal shows the destination of the proposed project, it is, therefore, a basis towards developing an acceptable project proposal. Next footstep in process is defining objectives that would help in achieving the goal. Program managers should not overlook both these steps, as, well drafted goals and objectives facilitate in developing an articulate proposal that has high chances of getting funded. A well written proposal always has clearly defined goal and SMART objectives to attain the desired results.

(a) What is a Project Goal?

The Project Goal is a broad statement that defines the destination of a project. It gives an idea to the reader of what problem your organization intends to address. It is a long-term purpose that the organization want to accomplish and reach in a specific time frame.

When writing a project proposal, great attention should be paid to the formation of Goals and objectives which have to be framed as correctly as possible.

The goal comes first in mind before starting writing a project proposal, because as the proverb says "if you don't know where you are going you can't know the way". Since the objectives are, the ways to reach the goal, therefore, the goal is the destination. This means, the project proposer/writer should have in mind, what the target of the project is and what is needed to be achieved. Should also determine and ought to be conversant on what does the project want to achieve. A project cannot contain many goals. There is only one goal usually in one project, but there could be multiple objectives that we want to achieve at the end of each stage or each project.

(b) Project Objectives

Objectives are the detailed statements describing the ways through which you intend to achieve the goal.

Project Objectives are the specific, measurable outcome of a program. They are the comprehensive but summarized aims for which the project works to achieve within a stipulated time. Many donors are easily convinced by specific objectives as they help address the problem stated in the problem statement section. Objectives should be specific: the more specific it is, the better to design activities, indicators and the Logical Framework. "If the objective cannot be measured, it will not likely be achieved." *(CORAT Africa 2012), Leadership and Management Training manual).*

One of your concern throughout your proposal should be to develop a logical flow from one section to another. Where as you can use introduction to set the context of the problem statement, you can likewise use the problem statement to develop objectives of your project. Meaning that; a defined **SMART** (Specific, Measurable, Achievable, Relevant and Time-bound) objective should offer some relief of the problem. They should directly address the problem mentioned in the Problem Statement. I must say here that "an objective is a "bullet" set to shoot and destroy the problem." Therefore, the objective should directly point to the problem relief. For instance, if the identified problem is a high incidence of drug abuse by youth in your community (substantiated, of course), then an objective of your program should be the reduction of the incidence of drug abuse among youth in your community. If the problem is unemployment, then an objective is the decreasing unemployment rate among the youth.

(c) What is S.M.A.R.T.

As stated above in the previous paragraph, SMART is an acronym of "Specific, Measurable, Achievable, Relevant and Time-bound". Literally, in the daily use, the word smart means to be keen or well dressed.

"Like many words in the English language, "SMART" can mean a number of different things.

Its commonest meaning is a kind of intelligence. It is more often associated with a knowledge of facts and memory than with wisdom or philosophical depth. Those two are more commonly associated with the word "wise." A smart kid is usually the one with the best grades.

It also has a meaning in fashion, describing either an item of clothing, makeup, haircut, or overall look. A hat or dress is often called "very smart," although I associate this meaning of the word more with British English than with American English". *(Mulder, P. (2018). SMART Goals. Retrieved (20th September 2019) from ToolsHero: https://www.toolshero.com/time-management/smart-goals/*

(d) SMART Project Goals

The concept of SMART Goals is used in a practical way as a powerful effective and time management tool. A SMART goal gives direction to what you want to achieve. In this way it will give a sense of direction to everyone who wants to achieve the goal and it is highly likely that it can be really completed successfully. A well-formulated goal is easy to understand for everyone. Below is an explanation of each of the SMART letters.

i. Specific

A goal must be specific in its aspects. Within a business arena; a vague goal such as 'our company wants to enhance its turnover 'indicates that the current situation is not satisfactory. Apparently, the turnover must be enhanced. However, there is not a real plan to realize this goal. So, it is unclear for all the parties involved what they should do. The SMART goals should therefore be formulated more precisely and specifically so that everyone knows what is expected from them. The goal must describe an observable action, behavior or result. It helps if a quantitative value is linked to a number, amount or percentage.

By answering the so-call 6 Ws - questions in advance, the goal will become more specific and concrete:

1.   What do we wish to accomplish?

2.   Who are involved?

3.   Which resources are needed?

4.   When is it going to happen?

5.   What parts of the goal are essential?

6.   Why is this goal important?

ii. Measurable

Each SMART goal has a starting as well as a finishing point and they are indications of the quality of efforts to be made. A system, method and procedure must mention which determines to what extent the target moment has been achieved. Therefore, it is advisable to have a benchmark and to determine a baseline measurement of the starting situation. The following questions will give a light if the goal you are developing is measurable:

1.   What was the achievement of the past year?

2.   How do you know whether the goal has been achieved?

3.   Where do we now start at?

4.   Where do we aim at?

5.   What more efforts are required?

6.   How can it be measured?

7.   Is the method to be used to measure the results compatible to the intended goal?

iii. Attainable/Acceptable

SMART goals must be attainable and acceptable for you as well as for the group or the organization.

Mulder, P. 2018, states that; "For managers, it is important to create support for the goal among the employees. Only then the goal stands a chance of succeeding. The support base will increase if employees are involved in the decision-making. This applies especially to short term goals. Therefore, Acceptable is also referred to as Ambitious; both go hand in hand and they should be in balance. Ambition is great when it is a motivator but it is risky when it causes deterrence. Meaning, if it brings down motivation, then the ambition is too high and as a result it stretches everyone to the limit". *(Mulder, P. (2018). SMART Goals. Retrieved (20th September 2019) from ToolsHero: https://www.toolshero.com/time-management/smart-goals/.*

iv. Realistic/Relevant

A realistic goal takes into account the practical situation and the work in which everyone is involved. It is impossible that everyone's focus will be on the same goal all the time; after all, there are always other issues requiring attention. For example, urgent jobs, tasks that need to be carried out and unforeseen events. Furthermore, the goal must be relevant to those who are going to work on it.

In addition, it must be ensured that, for the business firm, if the finance department is instructed to increase the income by 20% for example, then it will probably come to nothing. The marketing office, sales and field sales departments actually have the time and manpower to focus on the goal for a whole year. Likewise, within the organization, the goal must be challenging. If it isn't, it has a demotivating effect on the people involved in the project implementation and little or no attention will be paid to the goal with the consequence that the goal will not be achieved. Realistic is, therefore, about the feasibility of the goals. The objective must be challenging and bring benefits to the project staff involved. They must also have the capacity, resources and authority to get started.

v. Time-bound

It is especially important that short-term goals are formulated the SMART way. This is not always possible for long-term goals. Time-bound is often confused with measurable, but there is a clear difference between the two. Time-bound is actually about the time that is allocated to reach the goal. A SMART goal therefore has a clear starting date and a clear end date. A very tight deadline on the other hand has the demotivating effect and is, therefore, not acceptable. The sub-question 'when does it happen?' has in fact been answered under the heading Specific, for instance: from 1 January up to and including 31 December 2018, work is to be carried out to accomplish the goal. One year from now is not a SMART goal.

Mulder, P. 2018, contend that: "By setting a date and year for the goal, the organization can work towards this time limit. Incidentally, a year is a long period. By dividing the goal into sub-goals that have monthly or quarterly deadlines, everyone can work towards an interim completion. This enhances motivation and makes it pleasant to continue the work even when faced with adverse conditions". *(Mulder, P. 2018; SMART Goals. Retrieved (20th September 2019) from ToolsHero: https:// www.toolshero.com/time-management/smart-goals/*

(e) Differences between the Goal and Objectives

In most practices, some project writers and even consultants fail to distinguish between the Goals and Objectives. The two sounds similar in their context but there are big differences between them in a proposal and even in the common use. While a project goal is a long-term aim and general, objectives are short-term tangible realization of the project targets. Another difference is the number of each, while there should be only one goal in one project, but there could be multiple objectives in the same project. A project goal cannot be reached by one project, but the objectives are needed to be reached within one project. Increasingly, one goal can carry many objectives. Remember; the well-defined, SMART and practical objectives will enhance the chance of the proposal to be funded.

(f) Distinguish Between Objectives and Activities/ Methods

One common mistake in many proposals is a failure to distinguish between means and ends – a failure to distinguish between objectives and activities/methods. For example, many proposals read like this: *"the purpose of this proposal is to establish a peer-group tutoring program for potential drop-*

outs in the X area of Y location or country" or *"The objective of this program is to provide counseling and guidance services for delinquent youth in X settings"*. All the two objectives are not correct. The problem with them is because they don't speak about outcome! If a funder supports your project for a year, or for two years, and come back at that time and say, 'I want to see what you have done – what you have accomplished," what can you tell them? The fact that you have established a service, conducted some activities, don't tell whether you have helped to solve the problem which you defined. The funding source want to know what you have accomplished, to know the outcome of your activity, to know whether you have, though got into less trouble over the past year. Knowing that you have worked on it, is not enough. In that case, the objective should be accomplishment oriented. The former objectives above could therefore read like that; *"Reduction of drop outs from Y% to Z% through establishment a peer-group tutoring programme in the X area by December 2020"* or *"Decrease delinquency rates among the youth in the X area through provision of counseling and guidance services in the X location by December 2020.*

Some organization, trying to be as specific as they can, pick a number from the air as their measurable objective. For example, an organization might say that their objective is to decrease unemployment among the adults in the XYZ community by 10 percent. The question one can ask is where did they get that figure of 10%? Usually it is made up because it sounds good. It sounds like a real achievement, but it should be made of something more substantial than that. Perhaps no programme has ever achieved that high a percentage. Some funders might call it "an unattainable ambition. Perhaps similar programmes have resulted in a range of achievement of from 2 to 6 percent decrease in unemployment. In that case, 5 percent would be very good, and 6 percent would be as good as ever has been done. Ten percent is just very high and plain unrealistic. Putting such an ambitious target, leads the funding source to think that you don't really know the field very well.

Another difference that catch the writers is how to formulate an objective and an activity. It is wisely said that, an objective is the means to reach the goal and an activity is an action to be done in order to reach the objective and ultimately achieve the goal. By doing so, an objective has to be constructed without starting with "To." An activity is started with "To" because it is action oriented. You can say "Reduction" of unemployment among the youth; as objective and "To" train X number of youths in vocational skills as an activity.

Section 4: Strategies and Activities

(a) Strategies

Similarly, many people fail to distinguish between the Strategies and Activities. They tend to use one another interchangeably. A strategy is the driving force that capacitates the implementation process to achieve objectives. On the other hand, strategies are the means or mechanism that enables smooth implementation of activities. "Strategies are broad concepts or approaches to achieve the project objectives while activities are actions that are undertaken within these strategies. For example, 'building the capacity of the community members, is a strategy your project has adopted. An activity under this strategy can be: 'organizing training programs for community members" *http://www.fundsforngos.org/free-resources-for-ngos/difference-strategies-activities-proposal/*

(b) Project Activities

With the same logical flow, by now you have told the funder who you are, the problem(s) you want to address, your objectives which promise a solution to or reduction of the problems, your strategies which you want to use as a base for implementation. Now you are going to tell the funding source how you will bring about these results. You will describe activities and the methods you will use – the activities you will conduct to accomplish your objectives.

The consideration of alternatives is an important aspect of describing your methodology. Showing that you are familiar enough about your field to be aware of different models for solving the problems and showing your reasons for selecting the model that you have, give a funding source a feeling of security that you know what you are doing and adds greatly to your credibility. An objective might have more than one activity while a strategy might have only one activity and in this logic, you will be able to implement your activities efficiently.

One planning technique which you might want to use is this: Take a sheet of paper and divide it into two columns fold it downwards to make four boxes. The first column box is the "problems box, the second is headed "objectives,' the third "activities" and the fourth "evaluation." If you list all your objectives separately in the second column, you can then identify the problems that it relates to, the specific methods in your program that deal with the objective, and the criteria of success in reaching the objective as well as the method of evaluation. This helps you to see whether you are truly dealing with all of the problems you talked about, whether your objective is comprehensible enough to address them, and whether you have set up an evaluation mechanism to deal with your entire program.

Section 5: Benefits and Beneficiaries

It is not necessary for this part to be an independent section; it may be the part of other sections like rationale. But considering its importance for it gives a picture of what are the benefit targets and how many targeted beneficiaries are to be reached, it is better to form its own section or subsection as it will be an indicator at the end of the project.

The proposal without benefits does not give flavor to the reader on what will happen to the target community if one does not know their number and type.

On the other hand, a donor would like to know who will benefit from this project (Beneficiaries) and which type of benefits they will benefit. Beneficiaries are the people your project wants to reach and change their status through implementing your project. These can be affected directly or indirectly by the project.

Eva Wieners, 2016, states that "While beneficiaries are not typically listed in an overview parts of the proposal, information about the beneficiaries is actually very important in your proposal. This is because helping beneficiaries is the number one reason donors are willing to give money. Information about and references to beneficiaries should be dispersed throughout the entire proposal. This helps the donor to understand your project, see the importance you place on helping others, connect emotionally with the project and people, and finally decide if they support your plan. For these reasons, you should explain not only the number of beneficiaries you serve but also who they are and what challenges they face. In particular, you should directly state if your target group includes vulnerable groups of people, i.e. children, women, minorities, etc." *(Eva Wieners, 2016, How to write a proposal).*

(A) Direct and Indirect Beneficiaries

Generally, beneficiaries can be the people, groups, organizations, the Government and other structural systems. But, animals, plants, insects, the land itself and other living organisms cannot be beneficiaries. Below, you can see the distinguish between direct and indirect beneficiaries.

(i)   Direct Beneficiaries

Eva Wieners (2016), in her article on "How to write a proposal" defines a Direct Beneficiary as follows; "A direct beneficiary, sometimes called a primary beneficiary, is someone who is directly involved with your project and benefits from it. Depending on your project this could be people who participated in your training, students of the school you built or women who received livestock. The important thing is that the direct beneficiaries are connected with the project. Since they are so closely intertwined with the project, direct beneficiaries should be easy to count and describe."

(ii) Indirect Beneficiaries

Eva Wieners (2016), further defines that; "Indirect Beneficiaries who are sometimes called "secondary beneficiaries," as those not directly connected with the project, but will still benefit from it. This could be other members of the community or from the area or family members of the participants. Most projects are not planned around indirect beneficiaries, and so they are more difficult to describe precisely." *(Eva Wieners, 2016, How to write a proposal).*

Table No. 2: Direct and Indirect beneficiaries and their relationship

EXAMPLE OF A PROJECT	DIRECT BENEFICIARIES	INDIRECT BENEFICIARIES
Construction of toilets for 20 individual families	The 20 families that receive toilets	The entire community through improvement of general hygiene conditions

Conduct training for 50 farmers on how to grow trees in a soil erosion-prone area	The 50 farmers are the direct beneficiaries of the project	Communities living downhill are the indirect beneficiaries as their fields and water supplies are also affected by the erosion
Provision sewing machine to 15 women and train them in sewing skills	The 15 women are the direct beneficiaries of your project	Their families are the indirect beneficiaries, as the extra income the women will earn will benefit them as well

Source: *Eva Wieners, 2016, - How to write a proposal*

(A) The Logical Framework Approach (LFA)

A Logical Framework (or log-frame) is a tool used to link the project activities with the overall goal of any project. It is an analytical tool for objectives-oriented project planning and management. It allows the links to be identified and made explicit and allows project planners to identify and address potential uncertainties within a project. However, the project Objectives can be identified at different levels within a project design.

"It is a methodology mainly used for designing, monitoring and evaluating international development projects. Variations of this tool are known as Goal Oriented Project Planning (GOPP) or Objectives Oriented Project Planning (OOPP)". *(https:// en.wikipedia.org/wiki/Logical_framework_approach)*

A logical framework matrix is the output of a program design process where the programme staff work out how the program activities will lead to the immediate outputs, and how these will lead to the outcomes and goal. In an ideal world, a log-frame should be flexible and updated frequently. *(http:// www.tools4dev.org/resources/logical-framework-logframe-template/).*

Since most of project and report documents are very large and most of the project experts are always busy thus can't accomplish reading the volumes of these projects and reports, it has been practical to include the executive summary at the front page of these documents. Nevertheless, the summary itself does not give picture of a proposed project or the results of the project in case of reports as they not capture the major features of the project or report, particularly in respect of the various assumptions that have been made about the project performance or environment. Specifically, the executive summary may not adequately highlight the major areas of risk and uncertainty likely to be related to project performance, and the actions which are envisaged to ameliorate their effects.

In order to deal with this challenge, in 1970s, the United States Agency for International Development (USAID) commissioned a consultancy firm (Practical Concepts Inc.) to find a way of dealing with this problem and they developed the "Logical Framework". From that time, most of Funding Agencies and development organizations have more recently developed and adopted it as a practical methodology for designing, monitoring, and evaluating projects. (*UN Publications, 1974).*

However, the following should be noted:

1. The "Framework" should be brief, otherwise its impact is lost - a single page or less is the maximum allowed.

2. The "framework" emphasizes the importance of the clear definition of:

    (a) Objectives;

    (b) Means of measuring achievements objectively;

    (c) Assumptions which have been made in making forecasts of project performance.

3.   The "Framework" should be used right from the start of project preparation as a tool of planning, as well as being a **GUIDE** to the main features of the project at the front of a feasibility study or other reports.

4.   The "Framework" should be used also as a **TOOL** of ex-post evaluation, so that actual project performance after commissioning can be compared with the forecast in an orderly and systematic way.

Additionally, the Logical Framework provides a brief, systematic and disciplined approach which permits the identification of a hierarchy of causes and rejection of spurious assertions. At all stages of the preparation of the Framework, vague statements should be avoided, and as far as possible, targets should be quantified.

(C) Main Features of the Logical Framework

(a) Narrative Summery

The left-hand column is labeled the Narrative Summary and comprises the following:

i)   Goal

The programme goal is the higher objective towards which the project is expected to contribute. Individual projects are unlikely to be able to fulfill the programme goal alone.

ii)   Purpose

The project purpose is the specific results expected of the project, which in turn should contribute towards the programme goal. Clearly, the statement of project purpose is of importance to the way in which a project is both planned and evaluated. Projects frequently have more than one purpose, in which each should be expressed separately.

iii) Outputs

Project outputs are specific and direct results expected from project inputs and in turn, outputs are expected to contribute to the project purpose.

(iv) Inputs

Project inputs are the resources to be used by the project, i.e. staff, labour, materials, equipment, expertise, specialist services and financial resources.

(b) Objectively Verifiable Indicators

The following from left is a column for **Objectively Verifiable Indicators**. An indicator is a means of measurement which permits judgments about the situation. It is a measure that is used to determine whether or not a planned "result" or "change" has occurred. Indicators can be **direct indicators** or what are called **proxy indicators.** An indicator defines the performance standard to be reached in order to achieve an objective.

Objectively Verifiable Indicators (OVI) in the logical framework are real criteria for assessing project progress at the different levels shown in the narrative summary.

Objectively verifiable indicators must be Objectively verifiable - i.e. two independent observers should come to the same conclusion, and the results be communicated in an unambiguous way to a non-observer (third party). Indicators of project purpose, if stated precisely, can compensate for an imprecise statement of project purpose by supplying an explicit way of measuring achievement.

Indicators are quantities or conditions of the outputs identified in the narrative summary. These can be expressed as percentages, numbers, ratios, qualitative assessments or whatever is appropriate. In practice more than one indicator may be necessary. Indicators of inputs are also usually quantitative.

(c) Means of Verification

The third column on the far right, is for the means of verification, which are the instruments by which the objectively verifiable indicators can be measured. Each means of verification chosen should be associated with a particular indicator. The information necessary to measure the indicator is available from statistics, observation, surveys, in-depth studies. In its totality, the means of verification;

(i) Confirm if the indicators chosen are realistic since they specify how they are to be verified;

(ii) Facilitate project evolution by establishing in advance how criteria for success should be verified.

A wide variety of information sources will be available but before entering them on the logical framework they should be checked to ensure they exist and that they are valid.

When data collection is specified as a source for verification, it should be specified how the information will be gathered.

(d) Assumptions and Risks

Assumptions and risks are the tools used to analyze external factors which might impact on the project results. Important assumptions (found in the 4th column in the matrix), concern conditions which would affect the progress or success of the project, but over which the project has no control. This lack of control could arise from a number of sources, for example the fact those projects takes place in a natural environment and are therefore subject to natural variations. Another source or uncertainty arises from the actions of government such as policies, which may adversely affect conditions in the project in question.

Uncertainties may affect the causal links between, for example, outputs and the ultimate   project purpose. The outputs must exist before the purpose can be achieved. The existences of the output dose not, however, guarantee that the project purpose will be achieved – the occurrence of certain conditions may prevent achievement of project purpose. Hence the causal relationship between the project outputs and purpose should be explicitly stated a hypothesis – the evaluation – then checks to see if the hypothesis was valid. The core of the Logical Framework is the "temporal logic model" that runs through the matrix. This takes the form of a series of connected propositions

Fugure No. 2: Temporal logic model (The "IF" Model)

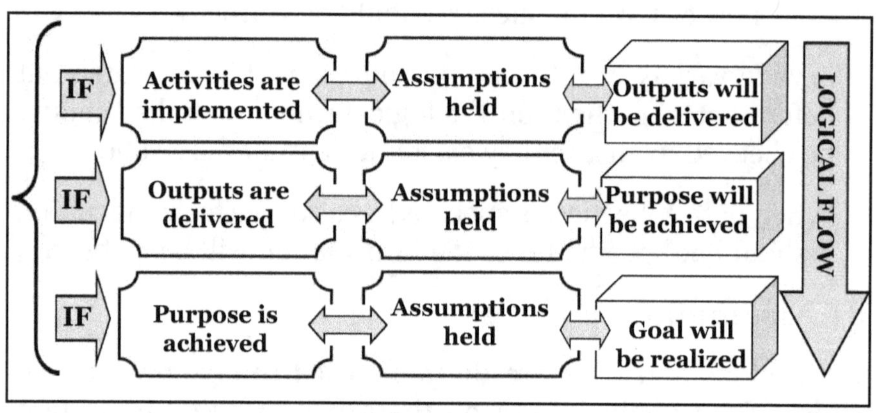

The "Assumptions" column is important as it acts as a connecting agent, clarifying the extent to which the project or program objectives depend on external factors, and greatly clarify **"force majeure"** of particular interest when the donor agencies at least briefly use the LFA as the essence of contracts.

These are viewed as a hierarchy of hypotheses, with the project or program manager sharing responsibility with higher management for the validity of hypotheses beyond the output level. Therefore, this is the essence of scientific method to non-scientific endeavors.

The LFA is also used in other contexts, both personal and corporate. When developed within an organization, it can articulate a common interpretation of the objectives of a project and how they will be achieved. The indicators and means of verification force clarifications as one would for a scientific endeavor, as in "you haven't defined it until you say how you will measure it." Tracking progress against carefully defined output indicators provides a clear basis for monitoring progress; verifying purpose and goal level progress, then simplifies evaluation. Given a well-constructed logical framework, an informed skeptic and a project advocate should be able to agree on exactly what the project attempts to accomplish, and how likely it is to succeed in terms of programmatic (at goal-level) as well as project (purpose-level) objective.

"One of its purposes in its early uses was to identify the span of control of 'project management'. In some countries with less than perfect governance and managerial systems, it became an excuse for failure. Externally sourced technical assistance managers were able to say that all activities foreseen have been implemented and all required outputs produced, but because of the sub-optimal systems in the country, which are beyond the control of the project's management, the purpose(s) have not been achieved and so the goal has not been attained". *(https:// en.wikipedia.org/wiki/Logical_framework_approach)*

Table No. 3: Sample of assumptions form at various levels

PROJECT ELEMENTS (LEVELS)	ASSUMPTION
GOAL	Political stability
	Inflation not too severe
	Equitable land tenure systems
PURPOSE	Incentives for change exist
	Related projects successful
	Government Policy commitment
	Replication successful
OUTPUTS	Permanent personnel positions established
	Long-term funding requirements budgeted for
INPUTS	Labour supply (skilled and unskilled) is adequate
	Funding will be timely

Source: *ICA Belgium 1994 – ITPDP Training Manual*

The existence of the output does not, however, guarantee that the project purpose will be achieved - the occurrences of certain conditions may prevent achievement of the project purpose. Hence, the casual relationship between project outputs and purpose should be explicitly stated as a hypothesis - the evaluation - then checks to see if the hypothesis was valid.

Table No. 4: The Logical Framework Matrix

NARRATIVE SUMMARY	OBJECTIVELY VERIFIABLE INDICATORS	MEANS OF VERIFICATION	IMPORTANT ASSUMPTIONS
Programme Goal:	Measures of Goal Achievement	How can the Goal results be validated?	Assumptions for achieving programme goal targets
Project Purpose:	Conditions that will indicate purpose has been achieved	How can purpose results be validated	Assumptions for achieving project purposes
Project Inputs:	Implementation Target (Type and Quantity)	Approved type and quantity of inputs used	Assumptions for availability of inputs
Project Outputs:	Magnitude of Outputs	Authentication of outputs tangibility	Assumptions for achieving outputs
Project Outcome	Medium term results	Validation of tangible project effects	Condition necessary for project result (positive or negative)
Project Impact	Long term changes caused by the project and other contributors	Validation of tangible changes	Static conditions necessary for changes

Source: *ICA Belgium 1994 – ITPDP Training Manual*

(e) The Advantages and Disadvantages of LFA

(i) Advantages of LFA

    a)   It provides a single statement of essential components of a project/report;

    b)   It presents them in a concise and systematic form, which reveals how the project is expected to work;

    c)   It clearly separates inputs, outputs and objectives,

    d)   It identifies external factors critical to the success of a project;

    e)   It sets down a comprehensive basis for subsequent monitoring and evaluation;

    f)   It acts as a focus for a multi-disciplinary approach to project planning and supervision.

Given that donor funded projects take place far from the headquarters of the funding agencies, and that they must be managed through intermediaries and the same staff are unlikely to see a project through from concept to completion, these advantages are especially attractive for Funding Agencies.

(ii) Disadvantages of LFA

    i)   There is always the danger that the Logical Framework Matrix may be used in a merely mechanical way i.e. people may simply fill in the boxes at the moment without seriously thinking through the problems.

    ii)   The setting of targets can lead to complications if they are not regularly reviewed and revised as the circumstances of the project or programme change. For example, auditors may find it convenient to use them as criteria of success in project implementation and if they are not kept under regular review the auditors could be badly misled.

iii) Because of the seemingly precise and "set" arrangement of the Logical Framework Matrix it may well lead to undesirable rigidity and inflexibility. Those with long experience in the operation of the system stress that it is only one tool among many and it must never be allowed to become a strait jacket. The Logical Framework must always be a servant of good project management and never became the master. For instance, if project managers believed they were going to be judged according to whether or not they achieved a given set of targets they might stick rigidly to achieving those targets rather than to exercising their proper function of being flexible and adaptive to changing circumstances and needs which meant that the targets were no longer appropriate and needed to be adjusted.

vi) There are potential dangers with quantified targets if they are wrongly used. Quantitative targets may lead to over-emphasis on physical output without regard to quality. There is also the risk that quantified targets may be set when they are not appropriate or may be wrongly linked to personal performance.

(f) Some Elements Found in the LFA Matrix and their Meaning

THE GOAL

This is sometimes known as a Development objective or the main or overall objective depending on the kind of project it presents. This is the main focus that the project is meant to contribute to in the long run, and explains the reason why the project is implemented.

THE PURPOSE

This is also known as an immediate objective. It is the immediate reason for a project. The effect which the project is expected to achieve if completed successfully on time.

THE OUTPUTS

These are the immediate results that can be guaranteed by the project as a consequence of its activities.

ACTIVITY

An activity is the action taken or work performed within a project in order to transform inputs (resources; funds, materials) into outputs (such as organizations, buildings) etc.

INPUTS

These include funds, personnel, materials, machinery and equipment of a project which are necessary to produce the intended output.

INDICATORS

In the context of LFA, an indicator defines the performance standard to be reached in order to achieve the objective.

MEANS OF VERIFICATION

The information necessary to measure the indicators is available from statistics, observation, records, surveys, in depth-studies etc.

ASSUMPTIONS

These are sometimes known as external factors. They are events or decisions which are necessary for project success, but which are largely or completely beyond the control of project management.

MONITORING AND EVALUATION

Although Monitoring and Evaluation has been put here as a separate chapter, but it is part of a project proposal. The funding agency would like to see how you plan to monitor or supervise your project as well as how you will assess the progress of implementation plus evaluating the outcome of the same. This part is very important because it shows the funding source that you are aware of assessing your project timely and at the end, the monitoring report will be compiled and make the flow of activities implementation.

6.1 Monitoring

6.1.1 The Meaning of Monitoring

Monitoring is a routine visit to the project locations for regular collection and documentation of information on project execution and its consequences and impact. It is a continuous process of gathering indications necessary for making suitable changes and adjustments in the project when need be as it continues. It is also a periodic inspection and follow up to the implementation of a project.

Monitoring is one of the project planning stages and it is done during project execution to assess the progress of implementation and its outputs. It is the systematic and routine collection of information from projects and programmes for four main purposes:

- To learn from experiences to improve practices and activities in the future.

- To have internal and external accountability of the resources used and the results obtained.

- To take informed decisions on the future of the initiative or project.

- To promote empowerment of beneficiaries of the initiative.

    Monitoring is a management instrument, this pre-supposes that; development programmes must be managed (not only planned). In regional development planning and management there are two important plans which are produced namely;

- The policy guidelines, and

- The development programme.

Basically, monitoring accepts the policy and programme design as given, it measures and records progress of implementation, it focuses on the compliance with the plan and is, therefore, by definition a continuous task during the whole life cycle of a policy and programme.

Monitoring is usually part of an overall management information system and it must produce necessary data or information on time. This requires the timely collection and analysis, planning and implementation of the development policy programme.

Monitoring is the provision of information and the use of information to enable the management to assess PROGRESS of implementation and timely decision to ensure that PROGRESS is maintained according to SCHEDULE. Monitoring assesses whether project INPUTS are being delivered, are being used as intended, and are having the INITIAL EFFECTS as planned.

Monitoring is an internal project activity, an essential part of good management practice and therefore an integral part of day-to-day management.

"Monitoring concerns itself with checking the progress of, among other things, the implementation it determines the causes of deviation from the plan and the initial effects (i.e. direct, planned, or indirect, unplanned effects) and impact (i.e. the effects of the programmed on the target group) of the implemented activities. That is to say, it provides the planner with the explanation of why things have happened the way they have, thus giving him the necessary information to do something about it, if necessary". ESAURP & ECD, (2009); *"CSOs Capacity Building Training manuals"*

6.1.2   Types of Monitoring

At the project level monitoring should include the following things:

i.   Physical and financial monitoring

Measuring the project activities and production of outputs against established schedules and indicators of progress. This includes recording of expenditure and checking that the expenditures are incurred according to allocated budget.

ii.   Process monitoring

Identifying factors affecting the progress of project activities and production of outputs.

iii.   Impact monitoring

Measuring the initial response and reaction to project activities and their immediate short-term effects. This type of monitoring is sometimes called internal on-going monitoring. It provides constant feedback to managers and staff so that corrective measures can be taken. However, Impact monitoring focuses on the following questions;

- What is the response and reaction to project activities?

- What are the immediate effects?

- What are unintended consequences?

- Does the intervention model remain valid?

Monitoring seeks to ensure that input deliveries, work schedules and production of targeted outputs and other required actions are progressing according to plan. It is an in-house, in-project and on-going activity.

Although monitoring and evaluation are viewed as related, they are distinct functions. Monitoring is viewed as a process that provides information and ensures the use of such information by management to assess project effects, both intentional and unintentional - and their impact.

Otieno, F.A.O. 2000, insists that; "Monitoring aims at determining whether or not the intended objectives have been met. Evaluation draws on the data and information generated by the monitoring system as a way of analyzing the trends in effects and impact of the project. In some cases, it should be noted that monitoring data might reveal significant departure from the project expectations, which may warrant the undertaking of an evaluation to examine the assumptions and premises on which the project design is based" *(Otieno, F.A.O. 2000, – The Role of Monitoring and Evaluation)*.

Monitoring is sometimes a recurring task already beginning in the planning stage of a project or programme. Monitoring can be used to document results, processes and experiences and can be used as a basis to enhance decision-making and learning processes. Also monitoring can be used to check the project progress against what was planned before. However, the data acquired through monitoring is used for evaluation.

Project monitoring exists to make sure you're implementing a project as competently as possible. It should always be a cohesive and constant part of project management, and vital decisions should never be made without it. Project monitoring is an important component of the project management cycle. It is one of the key ingredients in the success of the project. The project monitoring component must be included during the project initiation phase.

Brown, J. (2015), also commented that; "Project monitoring is not a one-time affair; it must be carried out continuously at different phases of the project. In most of the organizations, the projects are usually monitored by the project managers or team leads. It is their primary duty to design an effective monitoring mechanism that will keep a hawk eye on the project progress. It is observed that, organizations who don't implement an effective monitoring plan, find difficulties in understanding why their projects went wrong, and why it failed to create the desired impact, even though it was successful". *(Brown, J. (2015), - Top 4 Project Monitoring Steps).*

Project monitoring helps the implementors to see where or why projects fail. Therefore, it is a crucial element of all project management plans. It essentially comes down to keeping tabs on all project-related measurements, proactively recognizing possible problems and taking the necessary steps to guarantee the project is completed on budget, on time and in scope. Other writers also comment on the importance of monitoring. "Since project monitoring involves supervising all tasks and activities, failing to do it properly can limit the impact of successful projects. All-too-often project monitoring is glossed over – may be reviewed just enough to meet the obligations of a project management plan, or worse, discounted altogether. But project managers do so at their peril". *https://timelyapp.com/blog/project-monitoring-what-it-is-and-how-to-do-it-well*

6.1.3 Four Steps of Project Monitoring

Brown, J. (2015), explains on the steps of monitoring that; "The information about the ongoing project must be conveyed to the managers, supervisors, board members and stakeholders periodically. The information conveyed gives them a clear idea about the status of the project. Apart from the top level management officials, the information must also be passed to the project team members and also to other employees of the organization. This activity is generally taken care by the project coordinators or their supervisors. They have the responsibility to record all the developments that take place in the project from time to time. They can make use of two-way flow project monitoring, and ensure that the project is implemented in an effective manner". *(Brown, J. (2015), - Top 4 Project Monitoring Steps).*

Listed below are the four steps, that will help managers in monitoring the project effectively and efficiently: Adopted from: Brown, J. (2015), - *Top 4 Project Monitoring Steps.*

Step 1: Designing an Efficient Plan for Monitoring.

Designing an effective plan is the most important activity in the project monitoring process. Though, it might look simple, but there are lots of aspects which the project leader must consider while designing this plan. They have to identify the key areas in the project life-cycle that needs continuous attention. After identifying the key areas, project leads must set the targets that need to be achieved. Project leads must also take a note that, they cannot commit to a target which is difficult to attain. They have to set targets, that can be achieved by the team members. Project managers must also take a note of the resources that are available to them. These resources can be human, financial or technological. If required they must request for more resources. Apart from the outputs, project leaders also have to focus on the efficiency of their team and quality of the output.

Step 2: Designing Effective Report Management Mechanism

Project leaders can conduct meetings with the team members on a regular basis. This can be a formal meeting or an informal one. They have to ensure that these meetings take place at regular time intervals when the project team members will present progress reports of the project(s). At the end of these meetings, project leaders will have a clear picture about the project development, and also help them in identifying the problems that might hamper the progress or speed of the production process, and give them time to plan accordingly. They also have to keep an eye on the budget, and if they feel that the project might exceed the budget allocated, they have to pass this information to the top-level management. The project lead must also ensure that the team is performing in accordance with the specified deadline of the project.

Step 3: Recommendations for Project Improvement

This is one of the important activities in project monitoring. The project lead has to design a report management mechanism that effectively passes the information among the team members, top tier management and other people linked to the project process. This is important because the project leads get feedback and advises from the top-level management teams which will give him better ideas for the project monitoring process.

Step 4: Ensuring Guidelines and Recommendations are Followed Accordingly

Project managers must also ensure that the team is working according to the guidelines given by the client and also must see that the recommendations made by the top tier management team is implemented by the production team. Project managers or leads can also make use of technology for tracking the performance of their team members and give recognition to the top performers in the team. This will boost the morale of the team member and also inspire the other members in the team.

6.1.4 The Role of Monitoring

In defining the term monitoring, one needs to be exposed to a number of concepts associated therewith. **Otieno, FAO 2000,** stated that; "Monitoring is the continuous assessment of a programme or project in relation to the agreed implementation schedule. It is also a good management tool which should, if used properly, provide continuous feedback on the project implementation as well assist in the identification of potential successes and constraints to facilitate timely decisions. Unfortunately, in many projects, the role of this is barely understood and therefore negatively impacts on the projects". (*Otieno, FAO 2000, – The Role of Monitoring and Evaluation*).

Monitoring is not only concerned with the transformation of inputs into outputs, but can also take the following forms:

(i) Physical and financial monitoring

Measuring progress of project or programme activities against established schedules and indicators of success, also assessing the budget allocated against the out-put.

(ii) Process monitoring

Identifying factors accounting for progress of activities or success of output production.

(iii) Effect monitoring

This is also called Impact monitoring. It entails measuring the initial responses and reactions to project activities and their immediate short-term effects that will result in to long term outcomes.

6.1.5 Advantages of monitoring

The advantages of project monitoring include, but not limited to:

a. assess the stakeholders' understanding of the project;

b. minimize the risk of project failure;

c. promote systematic and professional management; and

d. assess the implementation progress and the outcome reached at the time of monitoring.

One needs to recognize the role played by the various stakeholders in monitoring. These players include the financiers, implementing agencies, project teams, interested groups such as churches, environmentalists etc. "It should further be recognized that, to be an effective management tool, monitoring should be regular, but should take into account the risks inherent in the project/programme and its implementation". (*Otieno, FAO 2000, – The Role of Monitoring and Evaluation*).

In many developing countries, one tends to find the following aspects in monitoring and evaluation of projects:

a. There is a dominant use of external consultants in monitoring and evaluation.

b. There is a dominant use of donor procedures and guidelines in monitoring.

c. Sustainability is often not taken into account.

d. Monitoring is sometimes used to justify past actions.

e. Concerns of stakeholders are not normally included.

f. Lessons learned are not incorporated.

If one looks at these aspects, it is clear that there is need to revisit them for sustainability. For example, over reliance on external consultants and donors may impact negatively on sustainability which is an important aspect of any project.

6.1.6 Decision-making in monitoring and designing the project monitoring system

The purpose of this is to provide a conceptual framework that may be used in designing a project monitoring system. For a start, one needs to re-identify the purposes of a project monitoring system. It should be emphasized that, whereas a project monitoring system is a process of comparing actual use of inputs and completed outputs with planned use of inputs and planned completed outputs, the purpose of a project monitoring system is to provide information to stakeholders that can be used to make decisions during the implementation of the project.

"Through brainstorming, groups can identify the possible stakeholders in a project. Among these could be the beneficiaries, the project management staff, regional and national ministry officials and the donors/financiers. Once this is done, it is important that a clear plan of how to accomplish monitoring while ensuring maximum benefits is put in place." *(Otieno, F.A.O. 2000, – The Role of Monitoring and Evaluation).*

6.2 Evaluation

6.2.1 What is Evaluation?

Once the monitoring information is gathered; it is later being assessed. This gathering action is known as "Evaluation". Definitionally; Evaluation is an analytical and accurate assessment of the accomplished phase or an ongoing project/ programme. Evaluations gathers data and information which can make the responsible organizations to make strategic decisions and consequently determine the future of the project or programme.

Evaluations should help to draw conclusions on the five main aspects of the intervention which include:

a) relevance,

b) effectiveness,

c) efficiency,

d) impact and,

e) sustainability.

Information gathered in relation to these aspects during the monitoring process provides the basis for the evaluation analysis.

Evaluation of the program can serve two purposes for an organization; The program can be evaluated in order to determine how effective it is in reaching the objectives which have been established in solving the problems you are dealing with. The concept of evaluation therefore, is geared towards assessing the results of the program.

"Evaluations are independent assessment of the outcome/impact and relevance of the project, undertaken by external collaborators or by the project stakeholders themselves in the case of participatory evaluation. The purpose of evaluation is a combination of learning, guidance and control based on an assessment of what has been achieved by the project. The Evaluation is based on a review of existing information, discussions with all parties involved, and impact studies." *(NORAD – ISBN 82-7548-002-7)*

As stated above, measurable objectives set the stage for an effective evaluation. If there is difficulty in determining what criteria to use in evaluating the program, it is better to take another look at the objectives. They probably aren't very specific.

Evaluation aims to determine whether the project objectives set in terms of expected outputs, effects and impact are being, or will be met. This leads to assessment of the results achieved, and the lessons to be drawn for future improvements in a later phase, or in similar projects elsewhere.

Output levels are a measure of the input utilization by the beneficiaries. If the changes in outputs are considerable, they may be detected even during the implementation phase of a project.

In other cases, the effects, for example, on health, arising out of the provision of health services as an input may not be quick to appear. And the impact of such effect on the general quality of life of the community will, in most cases, be a slow-developing process. An evaluation system will require the development of a series of data commencing before the project is implemented and continuing well past the completion of the implementation period. "Unlike a monitoring system with its emphasis on rapid assessment, an evaluation system requires a longer time span before even tentative conclusions can be drawn." (*ESAURP & ECD, (2009); "CSOs Capacity Building Training Manuals)*

6.2.2 Types of Evaluation Methods

(a) Ongoing evaluation:

Ongoing evaluation is done within the programme. It challenges the design; it is used to draw conclusion and make judgments and it focused on the relevance. It tries to determine why things happen the way they do. In contrast to monitoring, it is ad hoc partial and can only produce tentative results because of variation due to time.

(b) From problems to solutions

Presently, monitoring and on-going evaluation systems are being reviewed because of the failure to be effective as management instruments. Most of the systems have been tried and tested by donors or aided projects in many countries to avoid mistakes made in the project system; being repeated in region development planning and management. It is useful to briefly examine the major problems affecting current projects in the development planning and management. It is useful to briefly examine the major problems affecting current project system it can be seen as a list of "do' and don'ts" in the literature, most of the problems identified in project monitoring and evaluation systems fall into the following categories:

i.   Psychological

The psychological component is often underestimated, mainly because passive resistance to a particular system cannot be quantified or effectively measured. System through their passive resistance (i.e. by simply delaying data inputs analysis work etc.) is the reason why this passive (or perhaps in some cases active) resistance takes that:

- Information may pose a threat to planners and those implementing the plans

- The information can expose deficiencies of operation or performance

- It reveals weaknesses in "management"

- It often disregards the human dimension

- It is seen as form of external control

- Staff are often not involved in the design of the system, and

- They are often designed for externally-financed development projects which underline European management styles and techniques.

    When designing a system, it is necessary to overcome these problems, how this should be done is to develop a monitoring and on-going evaluation system for development planning and management.

ii. Economic

These factors broadly encompass the volume of data collected and therefore, the expense incurred and the degree of confidence expected on the information gathered. The problems which fall into the economic category are:

- The overall lack of clarity on how much information is really needed

- The discrepancies among users on the value of the information gathered,

- The poor system design which produces too much data,

- The lack of agreement on the expected results and the means (both technical and financial) to measure these results, and

- The overall cost (financial, manpower and time) of the system are often underestimated

iii. Technical

When a system does not function properly, it is the technical reason which is most often mentioned by those involved. The most important technical problems typically encountered are:

- The lack of, or poor-quality staff available for monitoring tasks.

- The information needs are usually unknown by staff of a programme.

- The systems designed by specialist outside the programmes are not easily understood and accepted by staff.

- Analyzed data and information arrives too late to be used in making decision.

- The system often lacks flexibility and they are seldom, if ever, radically redesigned.

- The system becomes inoperable because no specific responsibilities are assigned, and

- There are organizational problems, and lack of time to implement the system.

iv. Political

There are also political factors which can torpedo the existing systems, these includes:

- The simple fact that the results are often not acted upon, and

- Politicians' sensitivity to the implications of the system that may produce in respect of their role in the community

(c) Ex-ante, terminal and ex-post evaluation

All studies which are undertaken in the analysis phase, such as pre-feasibility studies, feasibility studies and so on, are all part of the ex-ante evaluation.

The evaluation determines whether the intended result has been achieved or not and reason why after the completion of the programme. However, "terminal" means evaluation conducted immediately after completion of the programme, and "ex-post evaluation" means some years after completion of the programme). It also, involves the analysis of the results reached with the base of the planned objectives and goals.

(d) Subjective and Objective Evaluations

Some development practitioners think Subjective and Objective Evaluations are the same. It is important to know the difference between the two types of evaluation:

(i) Subjective evaluation

Subjective evaluation of programs are rarely evaluations at all. They may tell you how people feel about a program, but seldom deal with the concrete results of a program. For instance, if we use an example of evaluation of the educational program that surveyed opinions about program success held by students, parents, teachers and administrators of the program. This is a pretty "soft" evaluation, and doesn't really give much evidence to support the tangible results of such a program.

In addition, this particular evaluation solicited comments from students when they completed the program, failing to deal with over 50 percent of the students who started but did not complete the program. Clearly, those students who finished the program are going to react differently, as a group, from those who didn't complete the program. And we might, as an agency, learn a great deal from those who didn't finish. From the nature of this evaluation, one might suppose that the educational institution involved was committed to producing what they thought would look like a good evaluation, but it wouldn't pass muster with a critical reviewer.

However, Subjectivity is introducing own biases into an evaluation and will often come in when the own programs are evaluated. Particularly if the continued funding will sorely depend on producing what looks like a good evaluation. This type of evaluation, normally gives biased results.

(ii) Objective evaluations

One way of obtaining a more objective evaluation and sometimes a more professionally prepared evaluation, is to look an outside organization or firm to conduct an evaluation for you. You might go to other non-profit agencies, colleges and universities in your community which will work with you in developing an evaluation for your program. Sometimes it is possible to get an outside organization to develop an evaluation design and proposal for evaluation that can be submitted to a funding source, complete with its own budget, along with your proposal. This not only can guarantee a more objective evaluation, but can also add to the credibility of your total application, since you have borrowed the credibility of the evaluating institution.

It is essential to build your evaluation into your proposal and to be prepared to implement your evaluation at the same time that you start your program, or before. If you want to determine change along some dimension, then you have got to show where your clients have come from. It is very difficult to start an evaluation at or near the conclusion of a program, for you usually don't know the characteristics of the people you are working with as they existed prior to being in your program.

6.3 Importance of Monitoring and Evaluation (M&E)

6.3.1 The Importance of Monitoring and Evaluation

The importance of monitoring and evaluation is broad, but in specific the following:

a) **Performance:** it helps the project team to assess its performance if the objective has been achieved and identify where have gone wrong or successful for lesson to learn.

b) **Accountability:** it is used to fulfill reporting obligations to other partners.

c) **Communication:** M&E when prepared help us to share results and experience with others.

d) **Learning:** from M&E we can learn from our achievements, failures (mistakes) and develop our capacity to perform better in the future.

Generally: M&E is an instrument that should:

- Facilitate a continuous process of all those involved in the implementation of a project through a "rolling planning,"

- Allow adjustment of program implementation at the appropriate level and through the responsible personnel,

- Improve:

  - ➤ The use of resources, the execution of activities and the achievement of outputs and objectives.

  - ➤ The size of and the reason for deviations between planned and actual performance.

6.3.2 Principles of M&E

There is no universally applicable M&E design. Its scope is defined by:

- The different units receding and using monitoring information and

- The type of information provided.

Any M&E system has to be tailored to:

- Type, complexity and size of project (e.g. sectors and regions of the project).

- Institutional setup of the project within the country.

- Relation between projects within the country.

- Managerial responsibilities at different levels.

- Conditions: - political, infrastructural, environment etc.

6.3.3 Interpretation of M & E Results

- If no deviations from the planning are found, or if those which are found are only small and thus acceptable, this confirms the correctness of the approach hitherto. There is no need for modifications and no intervention is required.

- If there are found to be deviations from the planning that can be attributed to aspects of the project's implementation, this means that implementation of measures has been better or worse than planned. The organization and scheduling of the activities and input of resources are modified and brought into line with the planning, implementation adjustments are required.

- If there are found to be deviations from the planning that can be attributed to inadequate planning of manageable factors (activities, resources, results/outputs), this constitutes a criticism of the planning carried out to date. The project's manageable factors are modified to take account of improved knowledge of the project environment, plan adjustments are required.

- "If there are found to be deviations from the planning that can be attributed to unrealistic planning, this places the whole project in question. Such deviations may be due to excessively high or low expectations regarding impacts at the level of the project purpose or overall goal. They may also be caused by changes in general conditions or external factors (assumptions). In such circumstances, the ongoing project approach must be continued. Where appropriate, proposals for new objectives and-at short notice-planning for a new project are to be elaborated in agreement with the clients. "ESAURP & ECD, (2009); *"CSOs Capacity Building Training manuals"*

6.3.4 *Steps involved in conducting M&E*

i.   Reviewing the planning documents e.g. project planning matrix.

ii. Determination of information requirements (information flow).

The following points should be clarified who/which project staff member require:

- what information

- when

- why (for what purpose)

- where (source of information)

- how (in what form).

iii. Recording the necessary information (what methods are suitable for collecting information).

iv. Analyzing and documentation of necessary information.

v.   Using the information project progress report as a base of assessing the current situation.

CHAPTER SEVEN

EXPECTED RESULTS, SUSTAINABILITY, PROJECT BUDGET, ANNEXES AND APPENDICES

The four sections mentioned above are also part of project proposal, although are put here as a separate chapter. When writing a project proposal, these four sections should be followed as one document of a proposal writing.

7.1 Expected results (Output, Outcome, Impact)

The funding source would like to know what is expected to come out of the project. It is better to explain here what will be the immediate results after conducting an activity (Output), what would be the medium results while the project is going on (outcome) and what change will the project bring about (impact). Outcome and Impact may be positive or negative depending on the assessment criteria or the actual results of a project/programme. This section is always an assumption part because it is where one would oversee the future results of the project that will be implemented.

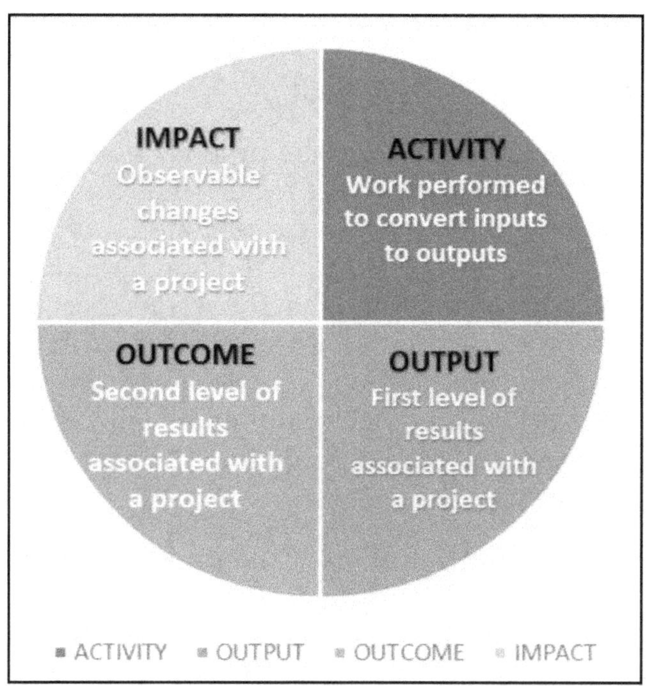

Figure No. 3: *Results characteristics quadrant (levels of results associated with a project)*

Difference between the levels of results

An activity has zero results at its start but delivers outputs. While output is the first level of results associated with a project which provides outcome, the outcome is the second level of results associated with a project and the impact is an accumulative result from the start of an activity to its end which must show changes, whether negative or positive. However, an activity must conceive inputs (material, human resources, equipment, finance etc.) in order to deliver outputs.

7.2 Project Sustainability/Future Funding

7.2.1 What is Project Sustainability?

Project Sustainability is how the organization maintains its capacity to continue its project even when the donor funds have reached its end. A project can come to an end, but its impact should continue. Therefore, the organization has to put in place a mechanism to ensure that the results accrued from the implementation of a project are sustained. This can be in terms like looking for future funding, stakeholders' involvement to create what is known as ownership and such systems which can keep the project wheel rolling while maintaining more results and benefits.

This is the last but one section of the project proposal, but by no means the extremely important. Ever more, funding sources want to know how the project will continue when their grant runs out. This is irrelevant for one-time only grant applications such as request for vehicles, equipment, etc. But if you are requesting program money, if you are adding to your projects through this proposal, then, explain how will you keep it going on after the funding end.

7.2.2 Features to be examined for Project Sustainability

Project sustainability will examine many features including:

a) Financial sustainability

This is how the financial resources which is needed to continue the project will be/is mobilized and available after the donor's funds has ended.

b) Organizational sustainability

This implies to the organization's capacity to continue functioning after the project end. Human resources remain active and motivated, material and equipment for the project continue functioning and more importantly, the organization itself maintains its credibility.

c) Community Sustainability

After the project end, the organization or implementing partner may leave and handle the project to the community. This community should have a sustainability spirit and therefore able and capable to carry out the project activities itself without dependence on an NGO.

d) Environmental Sustainability:

This is to ensure the resources used by the project are concerned with sustainable manner, protected and maintained and do not compromise the future generation. Meaning that, environmental sustainability as a crosscutting issue, should be observed in all stages of the project cycle.

7.3 The Project Budget

The project budget is not different to the general budget or organizational budget which is the financial plan that is designed to estimate income and expenditure for a given period of time. The project budget, therefore, encompasses the resources needed to implement the project, the source of revenue and how the resources will be expended.

The well-designed budget helps the organization to plan its activities while aiming at achieving the anticipated goal and acts as a catalyst to facilitate attainment of the desired results.

"The budget provides a realistic structure for making economic and financial decisions that are beneficial to the organization" *(CORAT Africa, (2012) – Leadership and Management Training manual.*

As with proposals themselves, funding source requirements for budgets differ, with foundations requiring less extensive budgets than federal agencies which sometimes need extensive and itemized budgets. However, there are standard budget formats that contains three types i.e. the operational budget which is sometimes known as the Recurrent Budget. This is a budget for day-to-day running costs of an organization. The second is the Capital budget which is the budget for procurement of long-term assets, furniture, equipment, motor vehicles and constructing buildings of an organization.

The third type is the "project budget" that involves all project implementation estimates. Sometimes, the Capital Budget may be part of the Project Budget, provided the costs fall direct to the project implementation. In most cases, the budget levels differ from one donor to another. Each donor has a standard that they offer according to their abilities and plans at that particular time. A project budget however, is the cost of project activities. Any cost featured in the budget, should be seen in the activities section.

7.4 Annexes and Appendices

The project proposal cannot contain everything you want your donor to know. This is because most donors receive many project proposals, therefore they need short but result oriented proposals. I order to do that, some documents can be annexed so that if needed, one can refer to them. Annexes can be but not limited to:

a)   Monitoring and Evaluation reports.

b)   Study/Research documents.

c)   Project Action Plan/Timetable (if not included in the project document).

d) Information/curriculum vitae of team members/project staff.

e) Photographs and maps.

f) Testimonies/quotes from beneficiaries and donors.

g) Cuttings from newspapers.

h) List of board members.

i) Audited Financial Statements.

j) A current annual report.

k) Proof of legal status (registration documents).

l) Constitution/Articles of Memorandum etc.

m) Bank details.

n) Recommendations from authorities.

o) Awards (if any).

In principle, not necessary that all documents should be annexed to the project document, but the project team will decide which one is essential to add on the organization's credibility. Some funding sources, normally mention which documents they want to be annexed.

7.5 The Covering Letter

This is always overlooked by many grant seekers. A covering letter is very important when sending a proposal to the donor. The letter should be written on the headed paper (letter head as you call it) of an organization which contains all contacts, the organization logo and should be signed by the top management i.e. the Chief Executive Officer or another head of the organization who is authorized to sign on behalf of the organization. The contents in the covering letter should explain what is the project about and who is responsible for implementation (the applicant). Remember, the "Covering Letter" is the first part the donor will read before reading the project summary.

CHAPTER EIGHT

VIABILITY ASSESSMENT OF A PROJECT PROPOSAL

Assessment tools are not part of the project proposal, but can be used as a guide to assess yourself when preparing a project proposal, because, the funding sources will use the same to assess your project application.

When assessing whether the project proposal meets the required standards, normally, a team of experts will go through the document and see if it meets the needed canons. The tables below are used to assess each section of a proposal.

Table No. 5: Viability Checklist and Assessment Guide of a Project Proposal.

Summary: Clearly and concisely summarize the request. WEIGHTED AVERAGE 10%	Yes	No	0-5	**Comments**
1. Identifies the grant applicant				
2. Includes at least one sentence on credibility				
3. Includes at least one sentence on problem				
4. Includes at least one sentence on objectives				
5. Includes at least sentence on methods and activities				
6. Includes total cost, funds already obtained and amount requested in this proposal				
7. It is brief				

1. Introduction Describe the applicant agency and its qualifications for funding (credibility). WEIGHTED AVERAGE 15%	Yes	No	0-5	**Comments**
1. Clearly establishes who is applying for funds				
2. Describes applicant agency purposes and goals				
3. Describes applicant's programs and activities				
4. Describes applicant's clients or constituents				
5. Provides evidence of the applicant's accomplishments				
6. Offers statistics in support of accomplishments				
3. Offers quotes/ endorsements in support of accomplishments				
4. Supports qualifications in area of activity in which funds are sought (e.g. research, training)				
5. Leads logically to the problem statement				
6. It is as brief as possible				
7. It is free of jargon				

2. **Problem statement or needs assessment** WEIGHTED AVERAGE 15%	Yes	No	0-5	Comments
1. Relates to purposes and goals of applicant agency				
2. Is of reasonable dimensions – not trying to solve all the problem of the world				
3. Is supported by statistical evidence				
4. Is supported by statements from authorities				
5. Is stated in terms of client's needs and problem-not the applicant's				
6. Is developed with input from clients and beneficiaries				
7. Makes no unsupported assumptions				
8. Is free of jargon				
9. Is as brief as possible				

3. **Program objective** Describe the outcome of the grant in measurable terms. WEIGHTED AVERAGE 15%.	Yes	No	0-5	Comments
1. At least one objective for each problem or need committed to in problem statement				
2. Objectives are outcomes				
3. Objectives are not methods				
4. Describes the population that will benefit				
5. States the time by which objectives will be accomplished				
6. Objectives are measurable, if at all possible				

4. Methods/activities Describe the activities to be conducted to achieve the desired objectives. WEIGHTED AVERAGE 15%	Yes	No	0-5	Comments
1. Flows naturally from problems and objectives.				
2. Clearly describes program activities				
3. States reason for the selection of activities				
4. Describe sequence of activities				
5. Describe staffing of program				
6. Describe clients and client selection				
7. Presents a reasonable scope of activities that can be conducted within the time and resources of the program				

5. Monitoring Present a plan for follow up of implementation of activities WEIGHTED AVERAGE 5%	Yes	No	0-5	Comments
1. Presents a plan for monitoring the progress of activities				
2. Presents a plan for monitoring and modifying activities according to the set time limits				
3. Informs who will be conducting monitoring activities				
5. Describes how progress will be assessed by data				
6. Clarifies which tools will be used to collect progress information				

	Yes	No	0-5	Comments
8. Explains how and when monitoring reports will be prepared and to whom they will be submitted.				

6. Evaluation Present a plan for determining the degree to which objectives are met and methods are followed WEIGHTED AVERAGE 5%	Yes	No	0-5	Comments
1. Presents a plan for evaluating accomplishment of objectives				
2. Presents a plan for evaluating and modifying methods over the course of the program				
3. Tells who will be doing the evaluation and how they were chosen.				
4. Clearly states criteria of success				
5. Describes how data will be gathered				
6. Explains any tool or test instruments such as questionnaire to be used				
7. Describes the process of data analysis				
8. Describes any evaluation reports to be produced				

7. Future Funding Describe a plan for continuation beyond the grant and/or availability of other sources necessary to implement the grant. WEIGHTED AVERAGE 5%	Yes	No	0-5	**Comments**
1. Presents a specific plan to obtain future funding if the program is to be continued				
2. Describes how maintenance and future program costs will be obtained				
3. Describes how other fund will be obtained, if necessary, to implement the grant				
4. Has minimal reliance on future grant support				
5. Is accompanied by letters of commitment, if necessary.				

8. Budget Cleary delineate costs to be met by the funding source you are applying to and those provided by other funders. WEIGHTED AVERAGES 15%	Yes	No	0-5	**Comments**
1. Tells the same stories as the proposal narrative (The budget is the cost of activities)				
2. Is detailed in all aspects				
3. Shows project costs that will be incurred at the time of the of the program, if different from the time of proposal writing				
4. Contains no unexplained amounts for miscellaneous or contingency				

	Yes	No	0-5	Comments
5. Includes all items of the organization asked				
6. Includes all volunteers' wages				
7. Details fringe benefits, separate from salaries.				
8. Includes all consultants with their costs				
9. Separately details all non –personnel costs				
10 Is sufficient to perform the tasks described in the narrative				

9. Attachments Are all there; are complete and are legible	Yes	No	0-5	Comments
1. List of board members				
2. Financial statements				
3. Audited Financial Statements (audited by a certified public accountant)				
4. Complete budget for the current year				
5. Complete budget for the immediately preceding year				
6. A current annual report				
7. Proof of legal status (registration documents)				
8. Constitution/Articles of Memorandum etc.				
9. Bank details				
10. Photographs, recommendations from authorities, awards etc.				

Source: *Grantsmanship Center, Brussels 1994: ITPDP Training Manual*

CHAPTER NINE

WRITING THE PROJECT REPORT

8.1 Meaning of a Project Report

A Project Report is a document which provides details on the overall picture of what has been done and the results thereof. The project report gives an account of the project prospects on how the proposed activities are being/were implemented during the project implementation or what are the results at the project end.

After accomplishment of the project activities and ultimately evaluation done, the following step is to inform a funding agency on what has been done and what results have come out. The funding agency would like to know if the funds they gave you have been cost effective, the intended goal achieved and if there might be a change as result of the implemented project. They would also want to know if their money has been spent according to financial standards and basing on the contract rules which the two parties signed at the start of a project.

A report can be delivered in spoken form (orally), sometimes in summaries, but a complete report is decent when presented in a written document. A report is therefore a document which contains information in an organized format to be presented to the specific audience such as the donors, government authorities and management boards. Report writing is a formal process of elaborating information on a certain issue and what has been done on that issue. The elaboration may depend on the audience or reader of that report.

8.2 Stages of project report writing

Reporting can be done at different time and stages during and after the project cycle as follows:

(i) At the designing stage, a project plan might be a report of its kind

(ii) During the project execution there are reports i.e. implementation report, progress report, monitoring report etc.

(iii) At the project end there is a project end report, evaluation report, or final project report.

Project reports will be required throughout all stages until an agreed point where the project has completed all scheduled tasks and/or outstanding issues are closed. Project Managers or Project Coordinators are responsible for reporting regularly.

8.3 Essential Information for Writing a Report

When writing a report, some information is essential to be included and this may include:

8.3.1 Title page

The title page normally is the front cover page that include information which describes in short form the name or heading of the report, the date prepared, and sometimes, the organization logo (if any) and other information needed to be on the front page such as the address of the reporting organization.

8.3.2 The Report Summary

The report summary is the general overview of the report document that describes all parts of a project report in a short form. It is a very important part of the project report because it is the first thing that a report reader will read. The report summary should therefore be clear, brief and precise. The summary should involve major points, conclusions, and recommendations. "Some people will read the summary and only skim the report, so make sure you include all of the relevant information. It would be best to write this when the report is finished so you will include everything, even points that might be added at the last minute". *https://grammar.yourdictionary. com/style-and-usage/report-writing-format.html*

8.3.3 Introduction

This is a part where you can explain the Project background and its historical concerns. Inform the readers about the commencement date, the funding agency and if possible, the objectives of the project. This part will also explain on how was the implementation progress and the stages the project has gone through.

8.3.4 The report body (Accomplishments/What has been done so far)

This part will show either the progress on what has been accomplished so far or the results accrued thereof as compared to the plan. You will inform the reader what mechanisms are in place to ensure the intended goal is reached and how the results will be ascertained. This part can include the insertion of photos and tables for clear elaboration.

8.3.5 Report Conclusion

The conclusion part is the summary of the report itself. However, the conclusion can be your own words, citing what are your ideas on the project implementation and/or what can be done to ensure the smooth positive results. It explains what has been reached and decided and the impact of that decision. The conclusion allows the writer to reinforce the main messages found on the report. Conclusion massages are the final words that a reader can go through to remind oneself of the entire report. Usually, the conclusion part touches the important parts and sections that you would like the reader to remind him/herself. Some people combine conclusions with recommendations, these are two different aspects as they serve different purposes.

8.3.6 Recommendation(s)

Report recommendation(s) are actions that a report writer suggest to be taken (if any) as response to what has been found and written in the report. The report recommendations can help the project implementors to fill a gap where it has happened and/or commend on what can be done to reveal positive results if such results were not reached during the past implementation. Conclusively, report recommendations are written as statements that describe actions to be taken as response of that report.

8.4 Ten Steps of Report Writing

(adopted from Open Polytechnic): (https://www.openpolytechnic.ac.nz/current-students/study-tips-and-techniques/assignments/how-to-write-a-report/)

(italics are the author's words "my own words")

Open Polytechnic recommends on the ten steps to be followed while compiling a project report as follows:

Step 1: Decide on the 'Terms of reference'

To decide on the terms of reference for your report, read your instructions and any other information you've been given about the report, and think about the purpose of the report. The following questions *(the 5 Ws)* will help you to draft your terms of reference:

➤ What is it about?

➤ Which exactly is needed?

➤ Why is it needed?

➤ When do I need to do it?

➤ Who is it for, or who is it aimed at?

Step 2: Decide on the procedure

This means planning your investigation or research, and how you'll write the report. Ask yourself the following questions:

➤ What information do I need?

➤ Do I need to do any background reading?

➤ What articles or documents do I need?

➤ Do I need to contact the library for assistance?

➤ Do I need to interview or observe people?

➤ Do I have to record data?

➤ How will I go about this?

Answering these questions will help you draft the procedure section of your report, which outlines the steps you've taken to carry out the investigation.

Step 3: Find the information

The next step is to find the information you need for your report. To do this you may need to read written material, observe people or activities, and/or talk to people.

Make sure the information you find is relevant and appropriate. Check the assessment requirements and guidelines and the marking schedule to make sure you're on the right track. If you're not sure how the marks will be assigned contact your *consultant*. What you find out will form the basis, or main body, of your report – the findings.

You may also refer to the monitoring report, evaluation report and the report from the Board of Directors (if any).

Step 4: Decide on the structure

Reports generally have a similar structure, but some details may differ. How they differ usually depends on the following:

➢ The type of report – if it is a research report, laboratory report, business report, investigative report, project report etc.

➢ How formal the report has to be and who shall be the audience.

➢ The length of the report and sometimes if there are instructions on the size of the report.

Depending on the type of report, the structure can include:

➢ A title pages

➢ Executive summary

➢ Contents.

➢ Introduction.

- ➢ Terms of reference.

- ➢ Procedure.

- ➢ Findings.

- ➢ Conclusions.

- ➢ Recommendations.

- ➢ References/Bibliography.

- ➢ Appendices.

The sections, of a report usually have headings and subheadings, which are generally numbered.

Step 5: Draft the first part of your report

Once you have your structure, write down the headings and start to fill these in with the information you have gathered so far. By now you should be able to draft the terms of reference, procedure and findings, and start to work out what will go in the report's appendix.

i) Findings

The findings are result of your reading, observations, interviews and investigation. They form the basis of your report. Depending on the type of report you are writing, you may also wish to include photos, tables or graphs to make your report more readable and/or easier to follow.

ii) Appendices

As you are writing your draft decide what information will go in the appendix. These are used for information that:

- ➢ is too long to include in the body of the report, or

- ➢ supplements or complements the information in the report. For example, brochures, spreadsheets or large tables.

Step 6: Analyze your findings and draw conclusions

The conclusion is where you analyze your findings and interpret what you have found. To do this, read through your findings and ask yourself the following questions:

- ➢ What have I found?

- ➢ What's significant or important about my findings?

- ➢ What do my findings suggest?

- ➢ *How will the audience (reader) analyze these findings?*

For example, your conclusion may describe how the information you collected explains why the situation occurred, what this means for the organization, and what will happen if the situation continues (or doesn't continue).

However, all information in the conclusion, must base on (come from) the findings not otherwise. This means; don't include any new information in the conclusion.

Step 7: Make recommendations

Recommendations are what you think the solution to the problem is and/or what you think should happen next. *Recommendations are the instructions from the one who is compiling the report in own words. This also must base on the report itself, not otherwise.*

To help you decide what to recommend:

- ➢ Reread your findings and conclusions.

- ➢ Think about what you want the person who asked for the report should to do or not do; what actions should they carry out.

➢ Check if your recommendations are practical and are based logically on your conclusions.

➢ Ensure you include enough details for the reader to know what needs to be done and who should do it.

Your recommendations should be written as a numbered list, and *if possible*, ordered from most to least important.

Step 8: Draft the executive summary and table of contents

Some reports require an executive summary and/or list of contents. Even though these two sections come near the beginning of the report you won't be able to write them until you have finished it, and have your structure and recommendations finalized.

An executive summary, on the other hand, is usually about 100 words long. *(one to two paragraphs) or (half a page)*. It tells the readers what the report is about, and summaries the recommendations.

Step 9: Compile a reference list

This is a list of all the sources you've referred to in the report *such as monitoring reports, evaluation reports, the project documents, policy documents etc.*

Step 10: Revise your draft report

It is always important to revise your work. Things you need to check include:

➢ If you have done what you were asked to do. Check the assignment question, the instructions/guidelines and the marking schedule to make sure.

➢ If the required sections are included, and are in the correct order.

- ➢ That your information is accurate, with no gaps. *(and ore not yours, but from the references)*

- ➢ To ensure your argument is logical. The information you present should support your conclusions and recommendations.

- ➢ That all terms, symbols and abbreviations used have been explained.

- ➢ That any diagrams, tables, graphs and illustrations are numbered and labelled.

- ➢ That the formatting is correct, including your numbering, headings, are consistent throughout the report.

- ➢ That the report reads well, and your writing is as clear and effective as possible.

You might need to prepare several drafts before you are satisfied. If possible, get someone else to check your report.

8.5 Report presentation

If needed, the report should be presented to the responsible organs and authorities. While presenting, make sure the whole report is presented unless if the recipient directs otherwise. If this happens however, the report summary should touch all sections and the whole information should be featured. Always expect acknowledgement from the recipient, if not, then make a follow up to ensure if it has arrived and received.

CHAPTER TEN

RECOMMENDATIONS ON HOW TO APPROACH AND WIN A DONOR

The first impression is the base of success or otherwise. You may be communicating with the donor who doesn't know you or a donor might visit you for the first time to assess your capability after receiving your proposal and before they decide to fund your project. This stage is sometimes called, pre-funding visit, or due diligence, or pre-award assessment visit/meeting. If you make a mistake at this stage, then your energy and efforts on the proposal you wrote will end in vain. There are some ideas on what can be done to impress your donor, whether through your application document or at the first meeting with the donor or their representative(s). The following ten recommendations can trigger donor's impression and smile towards you, your organization and your project.

Recommendation 1: Introduce yourself and your organization (Build your credibility)

If it is a project proposal, it should be accompanied with a covering letter. This letter ought to be written cautiously. It should be convincing, without unnecessary jargons, open ended but hit on point, clearly specifying the facts you want to put forward. Avoid needless arguments like personal greetings and irrelevant stories to circumvent eye catch up of the reader that might jeopardize the quality of your project proposal. Make sure your first contact to the donor is containing your self-introduction, your name, position and the organization you are representing. This introduction should be short and to the point while setting the proper tone for the rest of your communication. Also, you can use the heading of the letter as an eye catch up. The Subject or heading, is the first line most readers put their first eye in any document. Don't ignore this line as it is this the first impression that will pull the reader; therefore, construct your HEADING/SUBJECT line as an existing as possible.

For the case of a meeting with the donor, one has to get prepared like a "job seeker" preparing for an interview. Your body and dress appearance are the first eye catch up. Your self-expression and mode of conversation is as well a brain hummer. Your self-introduction and presentation on what your organization's purpose, what it has done and what are the future prospects are the resounding tools to convince the funder that you are the right partner they can work with. Some organization managers prepare a complete presentation on power point to illustrate photos and tables for the audience in the meeting to see. Remember, don't panic, be confident on what you are explaining. If you are not sure on what to say to the donor, appoint one of your staff to do the job on your behalf.

Recommendation 2: Avoid errors in Spelling and grammar

It is better to proofread your letter before you send it to your donor. Double-checking is a good way to make sure what you write has no typing errors, spelling and grammar mistakes. When the need be, you can assign one of your staff/colleagues to double check your document. When sending a letter or email to a donor, make sure you check and double-check your writing. However, some donors do not take in to account spelling errors and grammar mistakes, they just stick on the concept of a project. Nevertheless, a good letter without mistakes and errors is an added value to your request.

Recommendation 3: Be polite but not a beggar

Make sure during your meeting with the donor or in a letter you are sending to them, you don't seem to force ideas. Don't put your interests and philosophies in the mind of your donor. Do not be too forceful or antagonistic in your discussion approach as this can cause negative consequences. Be polite but don't seem like you are suppliant. What is needed is ideas that will convince the donor to give. It is neither your cry nor supplicant voice will make the donor decide to give if other elements are not satisfactory. Since you both want to establish long term relationship, be friendly and easy to one another. The long relationship is established on the first contact with the donor not otherwise. Remember *"Slow and steady wins the race"*.

Recommendation 4: Don't be monopoly

Do not send a lengthy email or start on a long monologue about the great program you are running. During the meeting with donor, do not monopolize the discussion. Listen to their explanations, ask questions where you don't understand and listen for the donor to respond. Don't show them that you know better than them, even if this is a truth. You can learn much if you show them that they know better than you, but don't be driven by unrealistic facts. Try to use soft language to show them that you have knowledge on the issue you are discussing. For letter communication, avoid wordy letters as this may wipe out the meaning and narrow the appropriateness of the letter contents.

Recommendation 5: Accept what you are given, don't get biased

Some grant seekers think funding is just money, not material or equipment. Some donors would like to donate materials or equipment like computers, cars and machineries and advise to reduce their cost from the budget. Accept them as they are equally the same as that you would buy if you were given cash money. Don't tell your donor "that is expensive, I can get the cheaper ones" as this might make your donor doubtful on your integrity and trustworthy. Make good use of the materials you are given, don't feel it is a free *bona-fide*. Let money come next if you want to maintain continued relationship.

Recommendation 6: Be time conscious and avoid lateness to appointments

A Minister was fired by the President because he came five minutes late to the meeting. Some people may think this was a very miner mistake by the Minister, but as presidential appointee, couldn't have wasted his appointment authority's five minutes. *The integrity of a Man, is established by his time management.* Avoid, lateness, don't make unnecessary calls to the donor and don't make unofficial visits to the office of your donor as this is also time wasting. Remember time is money, and time is one of the most valuable resources.

Recommendation 7: Listen to your donor's instructions

Most funding sources establish funding rules or guidelines. They may give directions on the format of a proposal, implementation and monitoring procedures, reporting formats and deadlines etc. Don't be much know, follow their guidelines even if you feel your approach might be better. If you are not sure what to do, ask your donor and do what you will be directed to do.

Recommendation 8: Avoid Writing unprofessional emails

An email is often the first form of contact you initiate with a donor, so make it a good one. Have a clear and relevant subject line, use a formal letter format, professional writing, and grammar, and keep your email short and to the point. Follow general email etiquette and do not try to attract the donor's attention with "tricks" like writing in ALL CAPS or using larger, colorful font, etc. Avoid using unrealistic words and phrases like, "hi" "hallow" until when you feel now you are in good relationship with your contact person.

Recommendation 9: Keep organized

Before you hold a meeting with a donor, organize yourself, predict the meeting discussion and predict questions that could be asked by the donor so that you can prepare yourself psychologically and physically to respond to questions and become active during the discussion. Failure to prepare yourself psychologically may lead you provoke answers and sometimes present false discussions. However, it is not a sin to have notes on the note book or prepare a presentation on the power point. Having a colleague near during the donor meeting with you is an added value because, where you fail to get an answer of a question from the donor, your colleague can intervene and respond accordingly.

Recommendation 10: Make a follow up of your meeting agreements

After a meeting with a donor, remember to send a letter of appreciation for their visit and or for the meeting. Within that letter, remember to point out what was discussed and your conclusion as that will commit the donor on what you have both agreed. Most donors feel that you are responsible and serious for the business when they get follow up letters. Within your organization, share what has inspired from the meeting with your management team and key staff so that they are acquainted with the progress of your project application.

CHAPTER ELEVEN

FINANCIAL MANAGEMENT AND FINANCIAL SUSTAINABILITY

Finance is the blood of any organization. However, finances, like other resources, have to be not only mobilized but also managed and controlled.   Finances are always scarce and delicate. Without proper management and control, the functions become unsustainable thus causes the organization to be unmanageable and sometimes ruin.

The most important aspects in any organization or business is Financial Management (FM). In this scenario, competent and qualified staff with financial management skills are needed in any organization regardless the abundance of money the organization has. If there is no proper Financial management and control, the organization cannot reach its intended goal.

11.1 Meaning of Financial Management

Financial Management (FM) is the process of controlling and managing the use of funds or money in the organization or business. London School of Business and Finance (LSBF) 2018; defines Financial Management that: "Financial Management refers to the strategic planning, organizing, directing, and controlling of financial undertakings in an organization or institute. It also includes applying management principles to the financial assets of an organization, while also playing an important part in fiscal management". *London School of Business and Finance (LSBF) 2018, - Financial Management.*

Financial management also involves the following:

- Maintaining enough supply of funds for the organization;

- Ensuring shareholders of the organization get positive outcome on their services while reaching the intended goal.

- Getting optimum and efficient utilization of funds with result orientation;

J. F. Brandley defines Financial Management as "the area of functions management devoted to a judicious use of capital and a careful selection of the source of capital in order to enable a spending unit to move in the direction of reaching the goals".

TRACE (2006), defines FM that: "Financial Management, involves Planning, Organizing, Financing, Controlling and Reporting on the organization's resources to achieve the set goal. Financial Management is, therefore meant to help the organization to achieve its mission in an efficient and effective manner". (*TRACE, 2006, - Leading for improved Financial Management and Financial sustainability*).

In many incidences, NGO Managers think Financial management is only concerned with the financial department and therefore it is a task of the Accounts Section staff. This is not right because both sides, the accounts department and the organization management are both responsible for managing of finances. This happens even when the Managers ask Accountants if there is still some money for the work. This means, they don't know how much is being spent and how much is still in the custody.

Also, **TRACE 2006,** insists that "Financial Management is about planning and control of activities by financial means. It is not at all about accounts only. A Leader with a sound sense of

Financial Management enjoys using economic theory and insights, mathematics, system analysis, law, taxation and behavioral science". (*TRACE, 2006, - Leading for improved Financial Management and Financial sustainability*).

11.2 Meaning of Financial Sustainability

Financial Sustainability (FS) is the main strategic issue of any organization. Dependency to donor money is very risky as it makes the organization vulnerable while endangering the credibility and sustainability of an organization. Also, since external donors are not reliable all the time, dependence on them can bring a shock to the organization's existence. In order to avoid permanent donor dependence, NGOs should put in place strategies to maintain what they have received as funds and let them be available even when there is no external funding.

"Financial Sustainability (FS) is the ability to secure sufficient funds to ensure that the organization can achieve its objectives. It means a continuous balance between costs and income of the organization. It implies that costs need to be controlled and income needs to be assured" (*TRACE, 2006, - Leading for improved Financial Management and Financial sustainability*).

An organization without FS strategies, is like a leaking water in a bucket. However small the leakage is, the becket will become empty at times. In order to maintain water in the bucket, water replacement is needed all the time. For example, if the leakage is 100 mil liters (mills) per minute, then the replacement should be 100 mills per minute, that will maintain the level of water in the bucket. Here, the water is associated to finances while leakage is related to expenses. When you spend money from your budget, you need more money to flow in, otherwise the money custody will become empty at the end and that will be the end of the organization. Financial sustainability needs therefore, continuous flow of cash in an organization to keep the financial wheel rolling. This meaning maintaining the revenue (in flows) to balance with the expenditures.

Figure No. 4: The leaking bucket

The bucket needs replacement of the same volume of inflow water as the outflow leakage to maintain the balance. If the inflow is little than the outflow, at the end the bucket will remain empty. Same as the finance inflow in an organization, if the outflow is much than the inflow, the organization finance will at the end become unfilled.

11.3 Maintaining Financial Sustainability

In order to have sustainable finances for your organization, the first step is to have a financial regulation that will be translated in to Financial Accounting Manual. While the Financial Regulations is used as a financial policy of an organization, an Accounting Manual is to be used by relevant staff of an organization in their day-to-day accounting and resource control duties.

The second and important step is to develop a financial sustainability plan or strategy that will be a guide to keep finances flowing in.

The Plan/Strategy should contain the following:

a) **Suggestion on how to establish Income Generating Activities (IGAs):** In most cases, IGAs are controlled by the organization itself. Common IGAs may include; consultancy services, secretarial services, investments such as premises and equipment for rent, sale of books/ printed publications, videos and other businesses that may generate income to the organization.

b) **Promotion of philanthropy:** "The term philanthropy refers to; an act of showing generosity towards other people and a sincere wish to help them, especially by giving to poor people. "Caring or love for humanity." *(TRACE (2006) - Leading for improved Financial Management and Financial sustainability.*

In Tanzania and other areas of the world today, this is well known as Corporate Social Responsibility (CSR), which involves the rich companies in supporting social work at grassroot level. This may also include local fundraising and working with local givers such as local corporate sector i.e. local companies, local government councils, eminent people in the area who can give money for your projects and even religious institutions. It also needs expertise to have skilled philanthropists.

c)   **Sustainable Financial Management:** this includes spending the available funds sustainably. Making sure there is no any unnecessary expenditures and the available funds are used in a sustainable manner.

d)   **Recruiting proper human resources in the finance department:** This can also be avoiding conflict of interest in which some managers recruit relatives and or friends in the finance department without observing expertise and qualifications of these new workers. Without qualified staff in the finance department, there is no Financial Management and Financial Sustainability.

11.4 The Accounting System

The proper management of any development organization depends largely on the efficient management of its accounting system and finances. Accounting helps to record, clarify and sum-up the organization's financial activities. Its purpose is to provide information regularly regarding the organization's financial position. The accounts should, therefore, always be up-to-date. In small organizations the entries will be made daily or at least weekly.

11.4.1 The Accounting Documents:

A simple accounting system uses the following documents:

➤ **Cash transactions:** This includes; withdrawals (vouchers/ receipt), deposit vouchers, cash receipts which are prepared when there is no supporting documents and currency verification forms.

➢ **Bank transactions:** Bearer cheques, Cheques not crossed, Crossed cheques, Withdrawal forms-debit/credit advice, Signature cards, Bank statements etc.

➢ **Other Accounting Documents:** Invoices, Stock entry forms, Petty cash vouchers.

11.4.2 Keeping the Books of Accounts

The accounts are maintained in accounts books which record the financial operations (accountant entries). These should always be supported by accounting document such as:

➢ **Operations:** Deposits, Payments, Credits, Transfers, Withdrawals, etc.

➢ **Accounting Vouchers:** Bills, Petty Cash Vouchers, Statements, etc.

11.5 The Organization Budget and Budgeting

11.5.1 The organization Budget

An Organization Budget (OB), is the key management tool and mechanism that allows the organization staff to translate the programmes and operations of the organization into financial terms. A budget therefore, is a written **revenue and spending plan** which shows how much money is needed for the organization's work and if the organization has enough money comparing what is needed for the organization's functions.

The budget is also the means through which the available resources are apportioned and it enables the organization, to decide on the amounts required for the programme; reducing some expenses and increasing others. The budget is a protective instrument that determines both the limits that should not be exceeded where expenses are concerned and the minimum amount that should be earned as income. The budget however, is, an indispensable instrument which no individual, family or organization can do without. The more numerous the activities, the larger the means and more complex the budget. The budget can also help the organization to mobilize resources for realization of the programmes according to the needs and planned activities within the budget itself.

Akhilesh G. 2019, defines a budget as: "an estimation of revenue and expenses over a specified future period of time and is usually compiled and re-evaluated on a periodic basis. Budgets can be made for a person, a family, a group of people, a business, a government, a country, a multinational organization or just about anything else that makes and spends money. At companies and organizations, a budget is an internal tool used by management and is often not required for reporting by external parties". *Akhilesh G, (reviewed), Jun 25, 2019)*

11.5.2 Budgeting

Budgeting is a process used when planning how to spend money which is available in the organization. If the money is not enough, then your spending plan will fit the available or expected income to the organization for a specific period. Therefore, budgeting means forecasting, planning and most importantly, analyzing the costs of the activities of the organization.

The Accounting dictionary defines Budgeting as "the process of planning future business activities by establishing performance goals and putting them into a formal plan. In other words, budgeting is the process of making financial goals for an organization or a company and creating a plan to achieve those goals." *https://www.myaccountingcourse.com/accounting-dictionary*

11.5.3 *Preparing a budget*

What has been described so far is budgeting under "ideal condition" i.e. where a program is structured to meet the felt needs of the members and the community, a budget is then prepared to support the programme. In practice, however, budgets do not evolve in that way, more often an association gets funded through individual projects, do not generally evolve through the steps recommended in the ideal model. Projects adjust themselves to the needs of an organization or community in the course of implementation. They are fairly rigidly managed against an estimate of income and expenditure.

An organization whose activities are funded through individual projects should incorporate individual project budgets into a single consolidated programme budget and perceive each project as a part of a single consolidated programme. The preparation of a "programme budget" commence with the income and expenditure estimates of different parts of the programmes. Some parts of the programme will earn an income which can be used for financing other parts of the programme. A budget is a type of "forecast" and three problems that arise in the course of such forecasting are:

i. Not accounting for large amounts of expenditure or income due to inexperience

This means not having sufficient experience in this field that may be a very real problem. However, the problem can be solved or minimized by finding out the accounting methods to adopt from other organizations involved in similar operations or by designing a detailed accounting plan that will show each item budget accounts etc.

ii. The need to have accurate and reliable data

The best information sources of reliable data are the accounts of the previous years on which forecasts can be confidently based. In the alternative, one has to rely on the experience of others, which may not be applicable for one's own association since each organization has its own style of functioning.

iii. The link between estimates and efficiency

There is the risk of spending a great deal of money, to earn a meager income. On the other hand, for the same amount of work, the cost can vary largely, depending on how efficient the work is carried out.

Therefore, each organization should work out its annual budget and include in it each and every activity and project which has been planned. To work out a budget, start with the income expected for the coming year. "If it is really impossible to estimate the income, even approximately, then the Management of the organization will have to be on the day to day system as a budget calculation will not make any sense. However, if, for example the organization knows in advance that two donor agencies are going to grant certain funds, and that a certain amount could be collected as membership fees, then it is in a position to evaluate the income and consequently estimate the expenses." *Vincent F, and Campbell P, 1989 "Towards financial Autonomy"*

11.6 Cash Flow

Cash Flow (CF) is the money coming in and going out (in cash) to cater for operational expenses of an organization. It is the growth or lessening in the amount of money a organization has. It is also to outline the amount of money that is raised or spent in a given time/period."

In accounting, cash flow is the difference in amount of cash available at the beginning of a period (opening balance) and the amount at the end of that period (closing balance). It is called positive if the closing balance is higher than the opening balance, otherwise called negative.

The level of cash flow is not necessarily a good measure of performance and vice versa. : high levels of cash flow do not necessarily ensure achievement of the programme objectives. In contrary, too much and unbudgeted cash flow can affect the performance of the project.

11.6.1 *Types of Cash Flow*

There are many types of Cash Flow, the Business Cash flow and the organization Cash Flow. The following four types of Cash Flow are more prominent to the companies and business.

i. **Cash from Operating Activities**.

Cash that is generated by a company's core business activities – does not include Cash Flow from investment. Statement of Cash Flow (also referred to as the cash flow statement) is one of the three key financial statements that report the cash generated and spent during a specific period of time (e.g., a month, quarter, or year). The statement of cash flows acts as a bridge between the income statement and balance sheet.

ii. **Free Cash Flow to Equity (FCFE)**

FCFE represents the cash that's available after reinvestment back into the business (capital expenditures). Free cash flow to equity (FCFE) is the amount of cash a business generates that is available to be potentially distributed to shareholders. It is calculated as Cash from Operations less Capital Expenditures.

iii. Free Cash Flow to Firm (FCFF)

This is a measure that assumes a company has no leverage (debt). It is used in financial modeling and valuation. Unlevered Free Cash Flow is a theoretical cash flow figure for a business, assuming the company is completely debt free with no interest expense. It's used in financial modeling to calculate a company's enterprise value.

iv. Net Change in Cash (NCC)

This is the change in the amount of cash flow from one accounting period to the next which is found at the bottom of the Cash Flow Statement. "A Cash Flow Statement (officially called the Statement of Cash Flows) contains information on how much cash a company has generated and used during a given period. It contains 3 sections: cash from operations, cash from investment and cash from financing."
Source: *https://corporatefinanceinstitute.com/resources/ knowledge/finance/cash-flow/*

11.6.2 *The organization Cash Flow*

The Cash Flow of an organization consists of inflows and outflows of the money in the cash box and in various bank accounts. However, there is a close relationship between the budget and the cash flow. If the programmes and projects are to be carried out as planned, then the necessary funds should be available at the need time to pay for purchase of materials, transport, salaries etc.

"To avoid problems, the cash flow of an organization should be estimated every month so that it could be decided how much should be in cash box and how much then should be in the bank to meet the expenses." *Vincent F, (1989) - The manual of Practical Management.*

11.7 The Strategic Plan in Financial Management and Financial Sustainability

A Strategic Plan (SP) acts as a guide and tool in the implementation of an organization activities in a participatory manner to address the intended issues. The Strategic plan normally focuses on the organization objectives, resources and opportunities for effective functioning and enhancing the organization's impact while scanning the environment in which the organization is operating, in order to identify her strengths and opportunities that can be fully utilized to hasten the realization of her vision. It also used to recognize her weakness and threats/limitations that may impede the implementation of the organization's programmes. Since many organizations operate in a dynamic environment, the SP has to be reviewed regularly to meet with challenges, periodical changes and new developments. Therefore, the strategic plan should have time limit. This means it has to operate in a certain period of time (say three years), after which, the review should take place.

In financial management, the Strategic Plan sets out what impact an organization aims to achieve among her target population over relatively long time with reasonably achievable funding. The organization should have a long-term strategic plan from which annual financial budgets will be prepared for the various operations.

From the financial point of view, the SP will show the following:

(i) a multi-year overview of proposed income and expenditures.

(ii) Broad trends and patterns of expenditure the organization expects to make to achieve its objectives over the envisaged long-term period.

(iii) A starting point for the organization Annual Budget for the following year.

(iv) A point of reference in long term financial tracking.

(v) Possible avenues for realizing funds to meet obligations on the plan.

A strategic Plan is, therefore, an important tool for both Financial Management and Financial Sustainability.

11.8 Financial Reports

Financial Reports are explanations of cash positions that is available with the Finance Officer from time to time. Reports are preparing as follows:

i) Daily Financial Reports

Cash positions available on the following working day.

ii) Monthly Financial Reports

These are prepared and presented to the financial officer/ payment approving officer, monthly, including Bank reconciliation statements, Budgetary Performance reports and Aged Schedules of debtors and creditors.

iii) Quarterly Financial Reports

These are prepared every three months filed with the following:

- Cumulative Budgetary Performance Reports, and,
- Fixed Asset Position reports.

iv) Semi Annual Financial Reports

This is furnished to the Management every six months of every financial year with inclusion of the following:

- Cumulative Budgetary Performance Reports.

- Aged Schedules of debtors and creditors for the six months.

- Draft financial statement showing financial position of an organization.

v) Annual Financial Reports:

This is prepared annually with the following attachments:

- Cumulative Budgetary Performance Reports.

- Draft Financial Statements showing financial position of an organization at the end of the financial year.

- Aged Schedules of debtors and creditors for twelve months.

- Fixed Assets Position at the end of the year.

- Progress Report on the past Audit Recommendations.

CHAPTER TWELVE

ORGANISATIONAL MANAGEMENT (OM)

12.1 Meaning of Organisational Management

In any organization of any size or complexity, employees' responsibilities are typically defined by what they do, who they report to and for managers, who reports to them. Managers are responsible for ensuring excellent work governance, identifying organizational weaknesses and role-modelling the culture expected. Specific structures are established to maximize and enable goals, objectives and plans to be executed in the most efficient and effective way.

Organizational Management (OM) therefore, is a management activity that aims to fulfill the organization's goal by handling adequately all the processes and resources available. OM is a discipline whose main objective is to plan, organize and execute activities that achieve the organization's pre-established aspirations.

"Organizational Management is a concept wide enough to cover an entire organization. It is also an activity that is normally carried out by senior executives who have broad knowledge and influence throughout the entire organization. This activity is frequently guided by a set of goals that must be achieved in order to fulfill the organization's long-term vision. By managing all the available resources properly, the administrators can guide the organization towards these goals."

(MyAccountingCourse.com (2020)
https://www.myaccountingcourse.com/accounting-
dictionary/organizational-management

12.2 The Deference between Organization Managers and Human Resource Managers

At some work places, the two positions are mixed up. Some think organization Managers or Administrators are as the same as Human Resource Managers. It is not true. Organization Managers are the Chief Executives who Manage the entire organization's functions while the HRMs deals only with manning workers and their functions. On the other hand, Human Resource Managers deal with managing workers through management of people within an organizations, focusing on policies and systems. The key responsibilities of NGO Managers however, are, to plan, organize, lead and control. Others will include coordination, staffing and evaluation.

NGO Managers in small and large organizations, from the South to the North, tend to adopt similar styles. They seem to spend most of their time solving problems, talking to their subordinates, taking decisions, participating in meetings, receiving visitors, receiving telephone calls, raising money and dealing with government officials. They do what is known as "fire-fighting" or "troubleshooting" techniques. Those who have some formal management training, occasionally and rather uneasily make some attempt to focus on planning and organizing, but very quickly the daily pressures and work challenges take over and they slip back into their old routines of "firefighting."

12.3 Organizational Effectiveness Checklist

In order to assess the effectiveness of the organization, the following aspects should be used as a guide and when worked on, the organization is liable to reach the intended results.

i)   The organization should have a clear vison, a well-defined sense of purpose and an effective strategy for achieving its purpose.

ii) The Organization should not be dominated by one of the founders and he/she should not take all the decisions on a very person basis.

iii) The organization should have clear and logical structures and administrative systems, based on the main activities or function of the organization. The staff have to know what their roles and responsibilities are.

iv) The organization should be financially secure with adequate financial management and sustainability systems, policies and strategies.

v) The organization should not be dependent on donor funding and the donors should not influence the organization's policies.

vi) The money received or collected should be used for the intended purpose and the management, therefore, ought to know where the money is going. The organization must have effective control and reporting system.

vii) There should be a significant turnover of staff, the salaries and benefits system ought to satisfy the workers and there must be in place adequate staff career and development prospect. Also, conflicts within the organization must be managed, ignored or suppressed.

viii) The organization must always be described as a "learning organization" by evaluating itself, learning from experience and adapting accordingly.

ix) The organization should always maintain the capacity, in terms of resources, special knowledge and organizational expertise to deliver effectively the initiated programs.

The above aspects have to be discussed by the Management Team and (if possible) among the entire staff team at a special workshop organized for organizational effectiveness assessment.

12.4 Management Characteristics of NGO Managers

There are three main characteristics, approaches, styles or levels of management of the NGO Manager which can be discerned as follows:

a) the manager as a fire fighter (unorganized)

b) the manager as the planner, organizer, leader and controller (organized)

c) the manager as an enabler, facilitator and motivator (a catalyst)

The implications from the arguments so far are clear such that the style or approach in level three is preferable and most realistic. However, apart from the management arguments, there is sound reasons for promoting level three approaches from the development perspective.

As we have already seen, most managers are stuck in level one. Nevertheless, it is essential that NGO Managers make the effort to get out of level one. They have to give a lot of energy and time to train their staff and establishing sound management systems in planning and organizing (level two) so that they can focus on their key role as facilitators (level three).

This has to be done in the full realization that crises will still occur and fires will still have to be extinguished out. So, part of the working day will always have to be devoted to level one and level two styles. But, if only Managers could give half the day to level three, a revolution in NGOs management practices will have been archived.

12.5 How to escape from the "firefighting" panache

Before discussing the need to escape from the "firefighting" style, it is worth asking whether the traditional management approach is still relevant.

The answer is both "yes" and "no." First of all, the list of basic management functions is not comprehensive. There are many others that can be added such as; problem solving, conflict management and resolution, communicating, time management and financial management to name but a few.

Secondly, these functions have to be carried out by everyone in the organization. All staff at whatever level have to plan, organize themselves, take decisions, resolve conflict and evaluate performance.

Part of the confusion stems from the fact that the term 'management 'is used in two different ways. The first one conveys the sense of managing yourself, your activities and your time. The second is based on the concept of the Director or CEO of an organization, a team leader or a supervisor of staff.

12.6 Organisational Functions

In order to reduce confusion, it may be more helpful to call the ordinary management functions (planning, organizing, controlling), organizational functions i.e. those daily activities that we need to do in order to make the organization operate effectively. This kind of functions, would allow the organization to redefine the key roles of the manager and its staff.

The manager's task is not necessarily to plan, organize take decisions or resolve conflicts, but rather to make sure that these things are done effectively in the organization. Hence, the manager supervises others and ensures that the key organizational functions are carried out. This line of thought helps to identify another overall management style: the manager as facilitator, catalyst, enabler, motivator and trainer of other staff.

12.7 Obstacles to effective Organizational Management

There are many obstacles that may impede effective management of the organizational workforce; the three mentioned below are very common:

i.   Insufficient resources to run the organization activities.

ii.   Lack of appropriate management skills among the Organization managers. Many managers prefer to rush around the whole day solving other people's problems without focusing on their workers performance.

iii. Low priority given to human resource management by NGO managers in which they put too much emphasis in fund raising than management of the available resources.

12.8 Development principles in Organizational Management

Most NGOs today accept the principles of community participation, people's empowerment and the need to build local institutions that can help the poor to organize themselves and to take responsibilities for their own development.

For many NGOs, these principles have remained at the level of rhetoric and there is little evidence that their development activities have changed very much in the field. One of the reasons for this is the fact that, the organization is still being run in a hierarchical, authorization, crisis management "firefighting" fashion. This contradiction cannot continue for much longer.

NGO leaders will have to practice the principles that they preach to the local communities.

In other words, development management (the management of the development process) and management development (the development of managers) have to be based on the same principles and approaches.

When presented with the need to strengthen organizations, field offices or departments, many people fall into the trap of looking for quick and simple solutions. So, more often than not, they send staff away on external training courses. A few have the possibility of organizing in-house workshops. Others prefer to change the structure or to overhaul the administrative systems and procedures. As strategic management is currently fashionable, some people prefer to organize strategic planning sessions.

12.9 Management for Organizational change

When planning an organizational change strategy, it is essential to think in terms of the four key components of an organization. Among the four, strategic planning and team-building are often the most important key components for NGOs. Therefore, interventions designed to improve strategic management and teamwork should normally precede training courses or revisions of the structure and systems.

There are, of course, many other important aspects of an organization such as; financing strategy, programme management, relations with the constituency and target groups, to name a few. These, however, will often be tackled naturally during the course of the strategic planning and team-building sessions.

Management is often defined in terms of such functions as planning, organizing, staffing and evaluating. Often, as a result, many trainings programmes focus on providing managers with the relevant skills for these functions. Thus, in many cases, NGO Executives are trained to become competent planners, organizers and evaluators.

Many people, however, argue that this interpretation of the managerial role is mistaken. Rather than actually doing the planning, the manager should be ensuring that planning is being done within the organization.

Although the manager often does take decisions, decision-making is not necessarily a managerial function. Instead the manager's role should be to make sure that the relevant decisions are taken at the right time, by a delegated subordinate, a team, the board of directors or by the manager himself or herself.

12.10 Managers as Facilitators and Coordinators

This view of management suggests that training programmes should be concentrating on a different set of skills for NGO Executives.   In this context, facilitation, coordination, Monitoring, problem-solving and team-building should be clearly stressed.

Even more importantly, the manager needs to have a very clear idea of how the organization itself works, how to identify problems and obstructions and how to select and implement change strategies.

12.11 Community Participation as a tool for effective Management

12.11.1 Meaning of Participation

Community in participatory approaches to development is often conceptualized as some kind of natural, desirable social entity imbued with all sorts of desirable values and the simple manifestation of this in organizational form.

In discussions of community participation, it is important to identify the appropriate definition of community. "When involving the community, it is essential to recognize that communities are not homogeneous but in fact heterogeneous" *(Mompati and Prinsen 2000)*.

Participation is therefore "a very broad concept that means different things to different people. The term is often used by people with different ideological positions, who give it very different meanings, that participation is an ideologically contested concept which produces a range of competing meanings and applications." *(Lane 1995)*, *(Hussein 1995; (Agarwal 2001)*

Community participation has become one of the cornerstones of NGO activities in development and, to a smaller extent, in emergency relief. Indeed, NGOs' supposed ability to mobilize local communities, is one of the main reasons for their current popularity among governmental and intergovernmental aid agencies. But in reality, the question is; how effective are they at ensuring the active participation of local communities in the programmes that they initiate, organize or finance?

Community participation theory is applied to a variety of situations, although not always appropriately. *Michener (1998)* suggested that participation has become a panacea. *Chamala (1995:6)* stated that 'community participation has been the hallmark of many successful development projects around the world'. *Michener (1998)* however posited that the term is widely applied in academic and project documents without regard for implementation realities. Even within the project cycle there has been varying applications of participation. *Estrella and Gaventa (1997)* identified that there has been a growing emphasis on participation at the 'front-end' of development projects in appraisal and implementation and now there is recognition of the importance of participatory processes in monitoring and evaluation of development and other community-based initiatives.

However, the few studies that have been carried out are often skeptical. In addition, many NGOs are becoming more conscious of their shortcomings in this area. Still, as NGOs are better at "participation" than government agencies and other organizations, the critics tend to be silent and such phrases as the "comparative advantage of NGOs" are spoken out.

Participation is generally considered to be one of the essential prerequisites for successful development and it is therefore, essential that the organizations improve their performance in this area. In addition, when the present enthusiasm for NGOs starts to diminish-as it inevitably will, their failures in community participation may well lead to a significant decrease in government support.

The most obvious obstacle area in community participation is the lack of skills. NGO Executives are often trained as project managers but they rarely have the ability to facilitate and catalyze other people's efforts. This is an area that needs improvement in the management cycle.

The lack of skills, however, is only the surface of the problem. Their basic attitudes and motivations are partly responsible. They see themselves as the educated experts, possessing considerable relevant experience and commitment. They need to achieve rapid and concrete results, and are easily frustrated with the time-consuming, erratic and sometimes unproductive process of community development. This also needs an open eye for change.

It is essential therefore; that they fundamentally reverse their attitudes and thinking towards the "target groups" (the term "beneficiaries" is very revealing) and become much more prepared to share and eventually to hand over power and responsibility.

Thirdly, NGOs are rarely based on participatory management principles. They tend to be hierarchical in structure and approach. Sometimes, decisions are taken at the top and handed down for implementation. They prefer working as individuals rather than as problem-solving teams. How then can we expect to be able to promote community participation in this situation?

A fourth reason stems from the project approach to development, which is counter-productive to participation as it essentially represents a mechanism for maintaining control in the hands of the donors and the intermediary NGOs. Community participation can only flourish within the context of programmes and institutional grants.

Finally, we need to clarify our own objectives in promoting community participation. At the risk of oversimplification, it is possible to identify four broad "levels" or "approaches" to participation. The first level could be the "in-kind contribution" approach. NGOs ask the community to make an in-kind contribution, usually labor or other locally available material and resources to the project. They forget that proper participation should start from planning through evaluation of the project. However, many NGOs have now moved away from this concept and today stress a second level, "the ownership" approach, emphasizing the importance of the community participating in the need's assessment and the identification of solutions as well in the planning, implementing and evaluating of the programme. Hence the ownership is placed in the hands of the community and the NGO sees its role as a catalyst, provider of technical expertise and as a source of funds.

Unfortunately, however, although many NGOs promote such an approach in theory, in practice they tend to oscillate between levels one and two and their attempts at mobilization are often seen as manipulation.

In addition, insufficient importance is given to sustainability, which is why a third level, which could be called "institutional development," is becoming more popular. The emphasis is now being placed on the creation or strengthening of viable and autonomous local institutions that are capable of carrying on the development process in a self-sustaining manner.

There is, of course, a fourth level; the "Transformation of Society," which relates to the logical extension of all community participation efforts. A radical transformation of society is based on self-reliant, self-determining communities. All NGOs, should seriously get prepared to promote participation at this level. They have to consider the implications for their own development strategies and for the motivation of the local communities themselves.

Hence, "Community Participation" is essential to development, we should therefore take it too seriously and hence, apart from major changes in our attitudes, skills, development strategies and organizational structures we need to clarify our objectives in promoting community participation.

CHAPTER THIRTEEN

HUMAN RESOURCE MANAGEMENT

13.1 Meaning of Human Resource Management

Human Resource Management (HRM) is the practices of managing people. It is an administrative approach of managing workers so that they deliver to achieve the organization goal. In many workplaces, there is a special department for management of workers known as the "Human Resource Management Department" (HRMD) and the heads of such departments are recognized as Human Resource Managers, as they are merely known in most workplaces as HRs.

Human Resource Management is really an action of managing workforces with an emphasis on those employees as assets of the business. In this context, employees are sometimes referred to as human capital. As with other business assets, the goal is to make effective use of employees, reducing risks and realizing the organization goal.

Being a strategic approach to the effective management of people in an organization, HRM is also designed to maximize employee performance in service of the organization's strategic objectives. "Human resource management is primarily concerned with the management of people within an organizations, focusing on policies and systems. HR departments are responsible for overseeing employee-benefits design, employee recruitment, training and development, performance appraisal, and reward management, such as managing pay and benefit systems. HR also concerns itself with organizational change and industrial relations, or the balancing of organizational practices with requirements arising from collective bargaining and governmental laws." *(https:// en.wikipedia.org/wiki/Human_resource_management)*.

"HRM is a product of the human relations movement of the early 20th Century, when researchers began documenting ways of creating business value through the strategic management of the workforce. It was initially dominated by transactional work, such as payroll and benefits administration, but due to globalization and consolidations, technological advances and further researches, HR as of 2015 focuses on strategic initiatives like mergers and acquisitions, talent management, succession planning, industrial and labor relations, diversity and inclusion. In the current global work environment, most organizations focus on lowering employee turnover and on retaining the talent and knowledge held by their workforce. New hiring not only entails a high cost but also increases the risk of a new employee not being able to adequately replace the position of the previous employee. HR departments strive to offer benefits that will appeal to workers, thus reducing the risk of losing employee commitment and psychological ownership." *(https:// en.wikipedia.org/wiki/Human_resource_management)*.

Ensuring that the organization is able to achieve success through people is the main purpose of Human Resource Management. Human Resource Managers organize the human capital of an organization for the aim of implementing policies and processes as they are set. They normally focus in developing employees, recruiting when necessary as well as maintaining employee relationships and benefits. Human Resource Development professionals always keep an eye on employees' training and constant development. This can be done through developing training programs, routine evaluations and rewarding best performance of workforces. Workers relations deals with the concerns of workers when procedures are not followed like causing workers' harassment or discrimination. To manage employee benefits must include putting in place compensation structures, maternity/paternity leave programs and other worker's benefits.

Margaret Rouse, (2014) describes Human Resource Management (HRM) as "the practice of recruiting, hiring, deploying and managing an organization's employees. HRM is often referred to simply as Human Resources (HR). A company or organization's HR department is usually responsible for creating, putting into effect and overseeing policies, governing workers and the relationship of the organization with its employees. The term human resources were first used in the early 1900s, and then more widely in the 1960s, to describe the people who work for the organization, in aggregate and other organizations of software to manage many HR functions." *Rouse M, (2014). Human Resource Management.*

Presently, there is a modern HR technology term known as "Human Capital Management" (HCM), which is now into more frequent use than the term HRM, with the widespread adoption by large and midsize organizations.

In organizations and other workplaces there should be strategy documents such as the Human Resource Management Policy, Staff Regulations and sometimes staff workers or personnel guidelines. Such documents, should specify the working environment of workers, terms of service, the workers' basic rights such as remunerations, Medical/health benefits, principles and ethics and other responsibilities and obligations of staff members as employees who are recruited by the organization, unless otherwise stated, defined and classified by the specific country's labour law. The documents set out the broad principles of human resources management for the staffing and administration purposes. They are, as known to each organization as may be, very imperative because they normally deal with workers' affaires, mainly in recruiting, regulating, development and personnel management as a whole. Each organization management has to make sure there is at least one of these documents, this will ensure smooth management and timely development of workers.

13.2 Assessing the organization workers

Workers are human resources who performs all functions of an organization. Workers have significant potential to the organization, therefore, assessment on what they are able to bring to the organization should be done technically.

The first step is to assign responsibilities for the organization activities, if you are using a team or otherwise. The point is that workers are an asset and there are things the organization can do to increase their value to the work. These people generally do not bring managerial training or experience to the job while they have learned by doing. It is important to remember, when you begin to look at how work is organized and the fit between workers and the positions they are in, because the managerial and supervisory jobs in your organization may look different from the same jobs in another organization.

For many NGOs; success is hard to measure because goals and results of activities and services are hard to quantify. The same is true at the individual level. Thus, workers are often unsure about what they are supposed to achieve, thus supervision face special challenges in making judgment about their performance.

13.3 Benefits workers bring to the organization

Every worker brings many things to the organization; some are easily described. While expecting to get something from what they are doing, workers also bring many benefits to the organization, such as:

- Skills and Knowledge: needed to run the organization and its activities.

- Spirit and their commitment to service: needed for successful accomplishment of work.

- Relationship: needed to build trust with the community, public officials, donors, clients and other local community members.

- Commitment: to the organization's goals and values that match those of the organization.

- Aspiration to advance: needed as it makes an ever-greater contribution to the organization and enjoy satisfaction from the job.

13.4 Improving benefits which workers bring to the organization

- **Express and use all of their talents:** This means placing workers in the right jobs, constantly encouraging them to do their best, rewarding their performance and enriching their jobs by allowing them to participate periodically in activities that go beyond the routine of their regular jobs, workers can use their talents fully and fruitful for efficiency of the organization.

- **Help them develop additional talents that they can apply in the organization:** This means training, counseling, exposing them to different parts of the organization and beyond. This may be additional to training while encouraging them to learn on their own.

- **Involve them in thinking creatively:** Give them freedom to think imaginatively about the organization challenge and suggesting ways to improve. This means gathering people together for discussions and listening carefully to what they say.

- **Use both staff and volunteers' talents**: These two groups share many things including their desire to serve, a multitude of talents, the need to be supported and rewarded. First, many managers didn't plan to manage; they are professionals; like doctor, nurses, midwives and other professionals who are in managerial positions because the organization need them or just appointed them. Most of them have inadequate or no managerial skills. When you use volunteers, some might have managerial skills which are important to share with other workers. Secondly, because NGOs' salaries are often lower than those of other organization and because of the environment in which many NGOs operates, it is difficult to compare for recruitment and keep highly qualified staff. "The potentially high turnover rate often affects the job structure with simple, limited jobs established so that new people can be brought on board quickly and without excessive training." *ICA, Belgium (1994) – ITPDP Training Manual.*

13.5 Making the most use of what workers bring to the organization

It is obvious that every individual worker brings qualities that are not reflected in a record of education and experience and these are not easy measured. Such qualities include intuition, commitment, a sense of humor, compassion, independence, an entrepreneurial spirit, common sense, integrity and many others.

It is up to the organization to take advantages of every thing the workers bring to it and to help them grow. There are many ways to do this; one is to make sure that the workers can express and use all of their talents. This means placing workers in the right jobs, constantly encouraging them to do their best, rewarding their performance and enriching their jobs by allowing them to participate periodically in activities that go beyond the routine of their regular jobs.

Another is to help them develop additional talents that they can apply in the organization. This means training, counselling, exposing them to different parts of the organization and encouraging them to learn on their own. Training visits to other places, are also useful strategies to make them deliver to their best. Yet another is to involve them in thinking creatively about organizational challenges and suggesting ways to improve. This means, gathering people together for discussions and listening carefully to what they say and or suggest for the organization's perfection.

Through assessment of your workers from various perspectives you can understand how effective your organization is; e.g. how they are organized, what their talents are, how well they perform and why and how well the organization develops and uses their talents and how it converts both staff and volunteers' talents for the organization effectiveness.

13.6 Involving workers in planning through Participatory methodologies

Another way of using your workers' potential is to involve them in the organization's planning processes using "Participatory Planning Method" (PPM) or the "Technology of Participation" (ToP). Participation methods have been the main driver of effectiveness in many organizations in which the staff have been part and parcel of the organization plans and functions. However, by definition; "ToP" is one of the group facilitation methods that was developed by the Institute of Cultural Affairs (ICA) of Belgium in 1994.

Participatory planning methodology is relevant because it:

a) is a structure for effective communication among the people with common interest?

b) generates creativity and new energy in a short amount of time.

c) infuses the planning team with a sense of responsibility,

d) catalyzes integrated thinking (rational and intuitive),

e) builds the practical group consensus and,

f) motivates the plan ownership spirit, thus building trust and support by all workers.

Additionally, Participatory planning methodology;

a) Provides for meaningful dialogue among the staff members

b) Broadens staff members perspectives

c) Allows people in the discussion team to become conscious of how their thinking can become actions

d) Directs the thinking of the group involved towards making a decision

e) It is adaptable to any situation and group

f) Results in clear ideas and conclusions and,

g) Allows the entire team of staff to participate while producing reflection and decisions based on all the available information.

Participatory Planning may include various methods, but to mention a few, includes:

i. **Discussion method**: This is a structure for effective communication. It is a process that can be used with individuals or groups. It is a tool that enables concerned people to initiate and take part in productive dialogue, it allows the entire group to participate and when used with sensitivity, it can enable profound sharing and unity within a group. Discussion method however, involves getting many people together and give them notions for discussion through four levels which are; objective (getting the facts), reflective (association of emotions and feelings), interpretive (gives value meaning and purposes), and decisional (where participants resolves for the future).

ii. **Workshop Method:** This is a common and very useful method in planning as it generates creativity and new energy in a short time. The method uses five steps i.e. "Context" which is setting the stage by setting the mood of participants for full participation, "Brainstorming" that includes generating new ideas through questions, ideas or issues written on the cards, "Organizing" the cards in order to push the intuitions of the team and form new relationships, "Naming" the cards according to clusters for discerning the consensus of the team, and "Reflecting" to the consensus for confirming the resolves and significance of products.

iii. Acton Planning Method: This method can sometimes go with the other two method because at the end, it can trigger the project start up. When it is done on its own, it concerns with discerning key actions that will be done, creating a calendar of actions and assignments for the project. Action planning has many steps including "Context" that set a stage by outlining the process of the method and time that will be used.

For an effective Participatory planning session, it is better to invite an expert in planning who can facilitate the methods until the final planning document is out.

13.7 Assessing the organization workers as assets

For proper function of human resources to make an organization effective, workers have to be assessed of their effectiveness in terms of performance and efficiency. This assessment helps the organization management to study six question as follows:

1. Are workers organized appropriately for the tasks the organization has to perform.

2. Are workers placed in jobs that take advantage of their talents?

3. How well do workers perform and how can you tell?

4. Are volunteers in jobs that take advantage of their talents?

5. How well do volunteers perform, and how can you tell?

6. How well does the organization use the creativity of its workers.

While exploring these questions, you will identify where the organization is strong and examine how those strengths can be used to achieve change in other areas.

13.8 Assessing how the work is organized

The purpose of this approach is to see how well the management of your workers fits what the organization does. The easiest way to do this, is to post a large copy of an organization chart on the wall for review.

First examine the chart to see whether or not it is current. If not, make whatever changes are required. Make sure there is some indication of how many people are in each position. If volunteers do not appear on your chart, add them in next to the staff they work with or assist, and estimate their numbers. Some may work only part-time. In this case, count a half-time worker as ½, a quarter-time worker as ¼, and so on. Now examine the way your workers are allocated in functional groups.

Explore the following kinds of questions:

1. In general terms, do we devote the highest numbers of workers to our priority tasks? If not, is there a reason? If there are differences of opinion among team members, discuss them fully.

2. Are there areas that are overstaffed or understaffed? Mark them with an "O" meaning Overstaffed or a "U" meaning Understaffed on the chart.

3. Look at your supervisors. Do you feel there are too many, too few, or a workable number? Why?

4. Are there tasks the organization does that are not reflected on the organization chart? If so, list them.

5. Are there tasks the organization should do but cannot be done the way workers are organized now? If so, list them.

6. Does today's organization chart match today's functions and tasks? If not, where are the inconsistencies?

Examine these issues in detail. Summarize the strengths of the structure in terms of using workers efficiently to get the important jobs of the organization done. Then draw up a separate list of problems that you see by developing a table with two columns, one for strength and another for problems.

Analyze those problems to see why they might, and identify things that you believe can be changed. Record your findings and conclusions carefully for use at the end of this exercise series.

13.9 Assessing if the workers fit positions

The purpose of this exercise is to see whether your staff workers have the necessary preparation, qualification and skills to perform their jobs successfully. In other words, you will determine how well the people match the positions. This can be done in three steps.

Step 1: Defining job requirements

First, draw a table on the form with four columns to identify needed number of staff at each position.

Table No. 6: Sample of workers requirement assessment Form (recruitment table)

POSITION	NEEDED	AVAILABLE	INCONSISTENCY
Technicians	3	2	1
Extension workers	2	2	0
Accounts section	3	2	1

Secondly, draw a "staff worker- position comparison table" and enter major job titles.

Table No.7:   Sample of staff worker- position comparison table

JOB TITLE	JOB FUNCTIONS (A)	SKILLS & OTHER CHARACTERISTICS NEEDED (B)	EXITING SKILLS & OTHER CHARACTERISTICS (C)
Technician grade 1	Technical engagement	Diploma in concerned technical skills	Certificate in concerned technical skills
Technician grade 2	Technical services	Certificate	Certificate in concerned technical skills

If you have job descriptions, you may be able to use them to list functions of workers in that position (column A) and the skills and other worker characteristics needed for the job (column B). It is important to focus on major categories of tasks rather than on each and every function the works has. If you do not have job descriptions, take a few minutes to describe each position and develop brief lists for entry on the chart. *ICA, Belgium (1994).*

The simple formula is; "Staff Required *minus* Staff Available *equals* Staff Gap" (SR-SA=SG).

Figure No: 5: The staff requirement assessment formula

The example figures above show that; the organization requires seven staff workers, there are five workers available, therefore there is a shortage of 2 workers in the organization. This means, two people are needed to fill the staff requirement/staff establishment.

Step 2: Determining what your workers bring to the job

At this step, you look at your staff workers to see what preparation, qualifications and skills they bring to the job so that you can later compare what you need to what you have. You will enter this effection in column "C". You may be able to draw on personnel files if you have them to find this information. Also, your organization may have a list of "entry requirements" for each job that you could use. However, when you look at the list, consider whether or not workers meet those requirements. If not, then adjust the list accordingly. When no reliable documentation exists, develop lists of skills, knowledge, experience and other attributes you believe your workers bring to each job.

Step3: Comparing your staff workers to what you need

At this step, you compare column "B" with column "C" in table No. 7 above, to see how well your staff workers fit the jobs they are in. Taking each job in turn, analyze the two columns for matches and mismatches (Table No. 8). The latter may include under qualified workers, overqualified workers or whose qualifications indicate they should be in a different job altogether. Summarize your conclusions in writing. Also try to assign a priority to each problem identified. The table below can be used to examine this:

Table No. 8: Sample of matches and mismatches assessing form for workers' positions

MATCHES	MISMATCHES	PROBLEM	PRIORITY

Review the conclusions carefully. See if you can determine why some of the mismatches exist. Ask yourself: Is it because there is no local training in the professions you need? Is it because the organization dose's recruit widely enough? Because some positions offer no advancement opportunities? In considering these kinds of questions, look at the matches in order to see why there are differences. Identify opportunities for change and save your findings for review at the end of assessment exercise. *ICA, Belgium (1994)- ITPDP Training Manual.*

13.10 Assessing the workers' performance

In this exercise, you are assessing two things: (1) how well workers perform and (2) how the organization evaluates workers' performance. This kind of assessment has six steps to go through:

Step 1: Seeing what kind of information is available

In this step, you identify what kind of information the organization has to assess staff worker performance and where that information is. While statistics are important, such as number of households visited or number of new acceptors enrolled, workers' performance may also depend on non-statistical indicators, like reputation in the community, ability to work cooperatively with others and the like. Therefore, do not restrict your attention to things that can be measured by numbers alone.

First, using the format that follows, list on the upper half of the worksheet all the kinds of information now collected and used, and where it came from. For example, number of households visited may come from a self-report, while assessment of ability to work with clients may come from a supervisor's report, verbal or written.

Second, develop a list of other information that is available, but not currently used. This might include client feedback or external evaluations. Enter it on the lower half of the worksheet.

Table No. 9: Performance information worksheet

STAFF WORKER PERFORMANCE INFORMATION WORKSHEET	
INFORMATION	**SOURCE**
1. Information now collected and used.	
2.	
3.	
4.	
5. Information available but not used	
6.	
7.	
8.	
9. Information needed but not available	

Step 2: Estimating staff worker performance

The purpose of this step is to make a broad assessment about how well the workforce serves the organization and it is clients.

Although you may review whatever documentation is available. In terms of performance evaluation reports, a thorough statistical analysis is not necessary. Using the format that follows, enter job categories in column A, and then rate performance, on a general basis, in column B using the scale 1 to 5 on the worksheet. Be as objective as you can. In the next step, you will be studying why performance may be high or low. At this point, you are focusing only on what it actually is.

Table No. 10: Performance information assessment worksheet

STAFF WORKER PERFORMANCE ASSESSSMENT WORKSHEET	
Ranking: *5 = outstanding* *4 = very good* *3 = acceptable* *2 = substandard* *1 = very poor*	
JOB TITLE **(A)**	**PERFORMANCE RATING** **(B)**
Chief Executive Officer	*4*
Operations Manager	*4*
Project Officer	*3*
Project Secretary	*3*

Step 3: Analyzing staff worker performance

This step will help you to examine why workers perform at the levels you determined. Develop two lists: (1) things the organization does to encourage performance and (2) things the organization does to discourage performance.

Table No. 11: Sample of encouragement and discouragement assessment form

TO ENCOURAGE	TO DISCOURAGE

Think carefully about how people act towards one another, physical working conditions, opportunities for reward or advancement, frequency and quality of supervision, the fit between workers and jobs that you reviewed in exercise 2, the broadest possible range of factors you can come up with. Next, develop a list of things the organization could do to motivate workers and encourage their performance.

Table No. 11: Sample of workers performance encouragement planning form

WHAT COULD BE DONE TO ENCOURAGE PERFORMANCE	HOW IS IT DONE
Motivation for workers	*Giving them good salaries, study visits, incentives, good working environment etc.*
Workers' development	*Put in place workers development strategy, giving them opportunities for more learning and on job training*

This might also include eliminating some of the "negatives" you have just identified as well as introducing new ideas. With regard to new ideas, stay as open-minded as possible, and not reject anything because you believe it is impossible or impractical. At this point, you are just developing options, not evaluating whether or not they are realistic options for your organization.

Step 4: Identifying opportunities for improvement

Using all the materials you have developed, summarize your findings in two lists, each in priority order: (1) categories where worker performance needs improvement and (2) things the organization can do to stimulate improved performance. Save these lists for later review. The table below can be used for this purpose.

Table No 12: Improvement needs assessment form

IMPROVEMENTS NEEDED	WHAT THE ORGANIZATION CAN DO

Step 5: Assessing how well the Organization uses its Workers

So far, we have been focusing mainly on workers in terms of their functional positions in the organization. We have also considered how the organization can affect how well workers perform in these positions. This exercise helps us look at another aspect of the relationship between workers and the organization, the extent to which the organization stimulates and uses its workers' ability to think about new directions, new approaches to doing things, and new ways to strengthen the organization's vitality. The objective of this exercise is to determine how well the organization takes advantage of the creativity within it. This is a very large issue and it deserves a lot of thought and discussion. This exercise however, suggests some practical ways to explore it. Nevertheless, this is also the time to use your organization and to be creative yourselves in identifying better ways to use the many talents of your human resources (workers).

Figure No. 6: Sample of Organization Chart

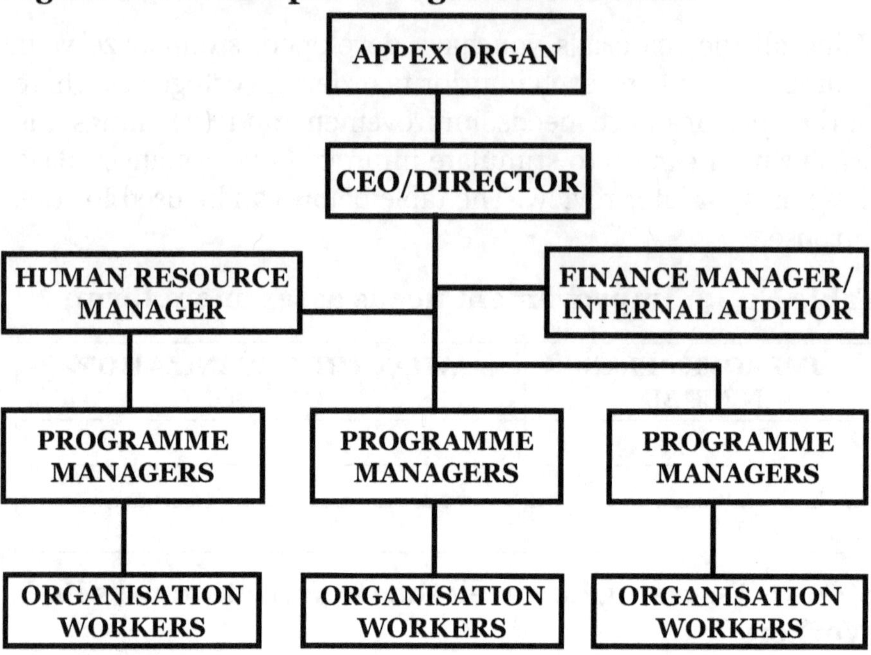

One practical tool is to refer back to your organization chart and draw lines on it showing how people actually communicate, not how they are supposed to commutate or how they report. Determine whether the communication between supervisors and workers is one-way or two-way. Also examine whether peers communicate with each other, within their units and between units. Study the completed diagram. See if the communication lines that now exist allow the creativity of individuals to be discovered and used.

Another practical tool is to rate the organization on characteristics that promote expression and use of ideas. For example, there must be opportunities to exchange and discuss ideas. Also, workers must believe that people will listen to them when they express ideas. Further, there must be a spirit of "give and take", where a new idea can be accepted in part or on a trial basis. Develop a list of characteristics that you believe promote expression and use of creativity. Next, rate your organization on the scale of 1 to 5 shown on the worksheet.

Table No. 13: Characteristics Rating Chart

CHARACTERISTICS RATING CHART	
5=highly developed *4=well developed* *3=adequate* *2=boney developed* *1=undeveloped*	
CHARACTERISTICS	**RATING**

Step 6: Summarizing Opportunities for Improvement

You now have a wide-ranging picture of how well developed the organization's worker assets are, and how well the organization uses those assets. This is the time to review all the information you have and summarize strengths and opportunities for improvement. Some areas are more critical than other and some actions will have greater effects than others. Reflect carefully on all that you have done and develop a list of opportunities for change, in order of priority, indicating what the expected benefits will be as results of these changes.

Table No. 14: Opportunities and Benefits

OPPORTUNTIES FOR CHANGE	BENEFITS

13.11 Human Resource Development (HRD)

As seen above, there are always gaps in Human resource management to fit the desired work performance among the workers. In most cases, these gaps are caused by the low capacities of workers. When this occur, then human resource development or capacity building is needed, in particular, this is building capacities of workers through training.

Human Resource Development therefore is developing the skills, expertise, competencies and knowledge of workers in an organization.

The concept "Human Resource Development" was first applied in 1968 in George Washington University and it was later used in Miami at the conference of American Society for Training and Development in 1969.

Heathfield, S.M, (2020) defines Human Resource Development (HRD) as "the framework for helping employees develop their personal and organizational skills, knowledge, and abilities, which in turn improves an organization's effectiveness. HRD is one of the most significant opportunities that employees seek when they consider you as an employer. The ability, and encouragement, to continue to develop their skills help employers to retain and motivate employees."

Heathfield, S.M, (2020) further insist that; "Human Resource Development includes such opportunities as employee training, employee career development, performance management and development, coaching, mentoring, succession planning, key employee identification, tuition assistance and organization development. *Heathfield, S.M, (2020) – What is Human Resource Development?*

13.11.1 What is training?

The term "training" has various connotations such as seminars, courses, exercise, conferences, workshops, lessons, group work etc. All these terms imply that somebody will initiate or organize a learning by others. To learn means to change behaviors with motivation from others. To teach, means to organize change of behavior of others. Training therefore means organization of learning for human beings or improving their capacities in a group or single capacities. It is the process of conveying knowledge and skills to an employee for understanding what he/she don't know or know little for better performance while doing a particular job. Training involves making employees accustomed with rules and procedures of the organization so that they may cope with all changes that occur in their organization.

Training is therefore, a process for organizing and equipping desired knowledge and skills to the organization workers for promoting effectiveness and qualities of employees. However, developing workers skills is periodical and should be given in specified time. Usually, it is better for the training to be given by a qualified expert in related field that require training.

Workers' Training is assisting employees to be active in their daily work developing their skills, knowledge and attitudes. Its main purpose is to increase effectiveness of workers to perform better and yield tangible results within and without the organization. Therefore, in order to ensure workers fully understand their responsibilities on job and their regular duties, Employers have to train them and make them adjust to the new position and perform to the desired output.

In this handbook we are talking about learning processes, which are organized for trainees in order to change their behaviors, to improve or correct existing behaviors, to improve knowledge and skills. The term behavior includes words like attitudes, opinions, knowledge, abilities and skills. Some of these changes can be observed but some may take place internally and, therefore, not able to be observed directly.

Training can be deemed successful if the trainees acquired knowledge, develop abilities and skills, form or change opinions and attitude in line with what the trainer planned. In the work performance arena, training can be considered successful if the existing gap within the work performance is filled.

Training doesn't just mean giving lectures or leading courses. The learning process takes time as it includes; repeated instruction, demonstration, problem solving by the trainees, practical experiences and successful application which are accepted, appraised and requested.

For a training activity to be successful it has to be carefully planned. The trainer should use the planning sessions to consider all the factors which may influence results of that training. Learning processes also take place in planning and working groups as they search for concepts, ideas, development of opinions, formulations of objectives, recommendations, action plans and solution to problems. Training means working with human beings and therefore psychological factors play an important role in the learning process.

The members of such training groups, however, are not referred to as trainees and instead of describing the process as teaching or training the word moderation or facilitation is used. Moderating/facilitation enables training participants to achieve their objectives through asking questions, discussions and team problem solving.

However, not all aspects of training can be planned for, it is not possible to predict how the trainees will react in terms of behaviors and spontaneity. The preparation phase therefore will be relatively abstract and static.

Learning is a complicated process which takes place under certain circumstances that are open to outside influence. To facilitate learning, a trainer must have a clear understanding of the factors involved for the training to be successful.

13.11.2 Training methods and design

In addition to correctly determining learning objectives and choosing topics and subjects well, the skilled trainer can utilize intrinsic motivation by many methods including the following:

i) Performance

This means: putting trainees into situations where they have to make decision and talk about their experience or to be confronted with lively action, not dead facts.

The trainer must be sensitive to the level the trainees are operating on. If the opening situation is too complex or contains too much new information which cannot be explained using existing knowledge or experience, the trainer will create difficulties.

ii) Motivation

Motivation refers to the power needed to push people to achieve something. Experimental evidence indicates that little learning takes place in the absence of motivation. However, what motivates one person may differ from that which motivates others. For some; the interest or challenge of the task is what motivates others. For others, the interest or challenge of the tasks is what motivates them. This form of motivation is called: Intrinsic, primary or factual motivation. For other people, motivation to learn is influenced by anticipated rewards or punishment.

"In the further process, motivation can be kept high by using illustrative material, changing the learning techniques, especially by using interactional methods and by avoiding boredom and frustrations. The trainer should show factual enthusiasm, should create positive attitudes towards the subject matter and should prepare the participants well for necessary efforts. Basically, the trainer knows how fact material can be learned". *ICA, Belgium (1994) – ITPDP Training manual.*

If learners expect reward such as promotion to a higher position, acquiring an official title or admission to a university, they are willing to learn; they are extrinsically motivated. However, it is sometimes impossible to employ external influences as incentives. This means' learning must be supported by intrinsic motivation. On the other hand, punishment can motivate people to learn because of fear of such punishment. For instance, if workers are informed that the requirement for the organization employment is a certain qualification, and those with lower level will be expelled from work, then all junior workers to that level will be motivated to learn to fulfil the requirement.

iii) Reinforcement

People need to feel accepted and respected by others. So, reinforcement and reward are always important aspects of the learning process in general, especially for motivation. A kind remark is a reinforcer, or a personal compliment or sometimes simply personal attention. The trainer should call participants by name and find ways to recognize their achievements using appropriate standards and noting progress. The use of exhibits and displays of outstanding work is a good responsive aid. Success is a great reinforcement, perhaps the best. In self-discovery techniques and programmed learning, success is a built-in reinforcer and motivator for learning.

"When the situation permits, the trainer should allow participants to work in groups and help each other, it will create a feeling of self-respect and of being respected, aiming and overcoming loneliness, isolation and competition. One of the aims of a training activity is to make people recognize the advantages and satisfaction to be gained by working together. This kind of reinforcement is always successful". *ICA, Belgium (1994) – ITPDP Training manual.*

iv) Feedback

In order to learn effectively, the learner needs to know if he/she has performed successfully; this may be confirmed by the trainer, by the reactions of the colleagues or by the learning situation itself. The more the learner knows about what he is doing, the more rapidly he is able to make improvements in his performance.

An effective feedback, must be given as soon as possible. If the learning situation can be arranged so that the learner is given a series of intermediate objectives and is provided with constant and precise feedback about his progress, the effect of feedback will be increased and will help to avoid monotony.

There are other different methods not described like case studies, role playing and discussion methods which are good illustrations of learning by early feedback. The best method of feedback is seen in programmed learning, where immediate reinforcement follows the participant's response to each segment of information. But, through question-answer periods, interpreting lecturers or through interactional learning, feedback is neither possible nor necessary.

v) Participation (learning by doing)

People learn in many different ways; by listening, by listening and watching, by trial and error, by observation and doing. Experiments prove that the more a trainee participates in the learning situation, the more effective the learning will be, particularly when is learning skills. If the participant is not called up on to respond and provide feedback for control and reinforcement, then learning will remain futile. Active participation is not only important for physical skills, but also learning by doing holds just as well for non-physical learning.

In order to make participation active during training, each principle in a lesson should be followed by carefully prepared trainee assignments and problem solving that make use of the principle presented by the trainer. Trainees must summarize, review, discuss and apply new material. They should translate new ideas in to their own words, or create ideas and pragmatic solutions to existing problems by themselves and not by the trainer. Training aids including working models and achievement tests that require interpretation of facts are effective aids to learning by doing.

Most trainees need to repeat a task several times before they remember it. Continuous repetition is necessary to consolidate what has been learnt. The trainer should therefore plan short summaries after each part or section of a lesson. This will entail the trainer repeating the material at intervals and instigating follow-up exercises and reviews.

However, learning by doing also means practice and/or repetition of behaviour to be learned which is necessary for remembering and for transfer of the classroom training to real life situation.

vi) Knowledge Transfer

Careful experimentation has shown that learning is easier when the learner can see its relevance or applicability to his own situation. Whenever possible, there should be a close relationship between the training programme and the work to be actually performed. Therefore, the trainer must provide suitable material and good learning conditions when presenting information beyond the normal scope of experience of the trainees.

The trainer should plan the training with regard to transferring subjects into practical applicability. The more experiences the trainer gives which relates directly to the trainees present or future experience, the sooner learning will take place.

The trainer should stress the underlying principles and ideas of what is being learned and make sure they are fully understood. Then the trainee will be more able to apply them to a new task or subject.

vii) Individual differences

The trainer must also take into account the differing backgrounds of trainees. Studies shown that Trainees differ in their:

- ➢ background (aims, fears, problems, satisfactions, social and economic needs, health, age, experiences)

- ➤ education (level of education, knowledge of the subject or related subjects)

- ➤ abilities (capacity to learn, capacity to do certain things)

- ➤ attitudes (working habits, intelligence, eloquence, understanding, social behavior and age insolences)

These individual differences demand a well-planned selection of participants in order to form a group which is as homogenous as possible. On the other hand, the trainer has to plan his performance around the individual differences. That means, he has to encourage individuals to make use of their best abilities and help them develop at their own pace. A good solution is working in small groups which have different working habits, different tasks and degrees of difficulties and different exercises. Special handling by the trainer is necessary when considering differences in age. Ageing slows down the perspective processes making it more complicated, therefore motivation for learning will decrease. Active participation in learning and sufficient relevant practice which is applicable to trainees' current jobs, will act to reinforce what has been learnt. These various factors in the learning process therefore become doubly significant.

Also, the trainer should help the trainees to see the affinity of parts of the subjects to other parts of the activity or to other subject matters which are already known by the participants. The trainer should improve the ability of the trainees to solve problems. Those who learn to solve problems learn methods of working and thinking which enable them to transfer new techniques to others.

Box No. 1: Qualities of a successful trainer

A successful trainer will:
- ➤ Always consider psychological facts of learning.
- ➤ Facilitate motivation.
- ➤ Reinforce appropriate behavior and give each trainee proper recognition and approval.
- ➤ Provide the trainee with information about his attempts to improve (feedback).
- ➤ Promote a meaningful integration of learning experiences that the trainee can transfer from training to the job situation.
- ➤ Provide active participation or interactional learning instead of passive perception.
- ➤ Provide useful repetition and appropriate excises.
- ➤ Adjust his performance to match individual differences in the group of trainees.

13.11.3 Preparing/Planning training activities

The proper training plan should comprise of nine steps or more depending on the type and length of a training activity itself. The diagram below shows the steps that must be followed in designing and running a training activity.

Figure: 7: Steps to follow when planning training activities

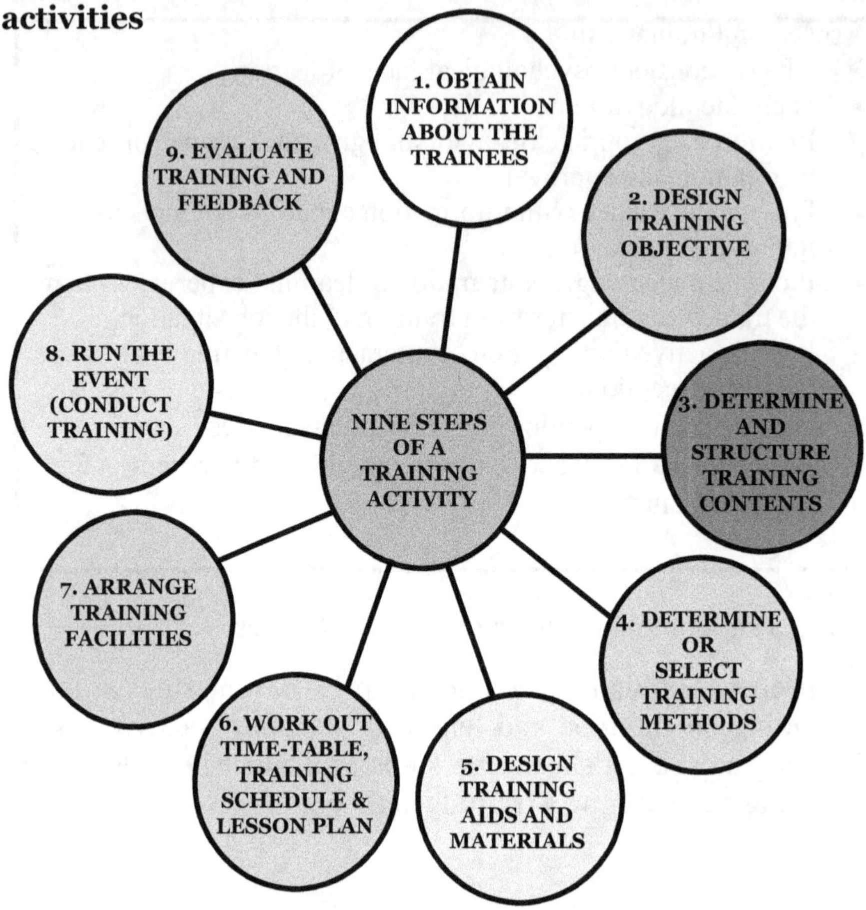

The nine steps can be analyzed as follows:

Step 1: Obtaining information about trainees and Identifying existing training needs

a) Obtaining information about trainees

The first step in designing training activities is to gather information about the people who will participate in the training programme (trainees). This will also include; to find out exactly who and how many people are required to learn and fill the gap at workplace. It will also help to determine the number and type of training activities needed. In order to find out what people should learn; it is important to determine the type of training activities presented. Additionally, to inquire into their background in details is an important part of the whole training process. The trainer must know thoroughly the background of a trainee so that when preparing training topics, they should fit the training needs of the organization and the trainees themselves.

b) Identifying existing training needs

For further details we have to identify the real needs of the participants. To design activities for indirect target groups the trainer must consider that individual training needs are derived from the situations experienced by the direct target groups. Undoubtedly these groups need to gain a clear idea and a better understanding of the life situation and the possibilities to overcome this situation.

The training needs of direct target groups, require similar planning. In designing activities for the first type group, it becomes clear that people need to be informed about the organization and the possible functions of its workers. In order to stimulate potential workers, activities should be designed which clarify the aims and objectives of the organization.

For the second type of group the main determining factor should be to enable the members to participate more actively in their organization work. The best method of determining training need is to formulate a questionnaire designed to be completed by the organization workers and clients/target group alike. Putting clients and workers together can be a valuable experience tool in determining needs as the written questionnaire can.

While training activities of type one and two of the organization training programmes are oriented on the role and function of workers, the identification of training needs for training activities for types three and four training programmes for the organization are based on job performance requirements. This means information on the training needs is obtained on the job. It is also true in identification of training needs in the field of small businesses.

The survey of job qualification should provide material which can be used to formulate training activities. The educational background of new staff must be identified and that information incorporated into training courses, workshops and other work related programmes. This may stimulate a programme consisting of two weeks of basic seminars followed by three weeks of practical orientation. Educational background e.g. school and university qualifications and related experience are also important consideration. This basic information can be obtained from workers' personal record, workers employment application letters, Curriculum Vitae, certificates, pre-tests and interviews.

Similarly, information on the qualifications of employees is needed, though this may be more difficult to obtain. One way to achieve this is by formulating a questionnaire asking which employees' need for training. The techniques, generally considered for assessing skills and abilities of employees are listed in the following sample chart:

Table No. 15: Performance and training requirement assessment form

PERFORMANCE REQUIRED	TECHNIQUES FOR ASSESSING PERSONNEL RESOURCES	THE TRAINING REQUIREMENT
Job analysis An inventory of job related and required qualifications for better performance.	1. Situation observation 2. Conduct interviews, 3. Review Workers' CVs 4. Make personal tests 5. Use questionnaires, and, 6. Analysis of operating problems.	All information of performance and demonstrated ability which are necessary for identifying training needs

Some comments and analysis on the above techniques for assessing personnel resources.

a) Situation Observation

Training requirements can be determined by observing the performance of each employee. A basic instrument of this technique is a chart on which qualifications for the jobs are stated and observations on performance are recorded. Hence, the training needs are identified. This technique can be handled simply in an organization where the number of employees to be surveyed is not too extensive. The identification of training needs is more difficult when employees from many organizations are observed.

b) Interviews

The same problem of qualification has to be considered when interviews are used to highlight training needs. However, if there is a chance of contacting a sufficient number of people with independent opinions, this technique has advantage because:

- It reveals attitudes and points of views that may not otherwise come to light. It helps to determine how people feel about their jobs.

- It facilitates expression of opinions.

- It reminds the worker on the importance to learn or build their capacities.

But; we also have to consider that information given in an interview may be highly subjective. Good interviews are time consuming and results are often colored by the interviewer's own attitude and their question techniques.

c) Reviewing workers' Curriculum Vitae (CVs)

The Curriculum Vitae of workers contains many information about the background and experience of a worker. Therefore, reviewing the CVs can show where the worker reached in terms of qualification and experience, hence determine what capacity building is needed to such worker.

d) Tests

Conducting tests of all types may be useful in determining training needs. These techniques are similar to those used in evaluating training activities. Tests can be used to discover training needs as well as to evaluate the effectiveness of training. However, this is also a highly specialized method. It is important to mention here that a lot of experiences are necessary in the administration and interpretation of test results to use this technique efficiently and hence to obtain adequate information on training needs.

e) Questionnaire

Another technique used to determine training needs is available in form of questionnaires. Definitionally, a questionnaire is an instrument that consists of a set of questions or other types of prompts that aims to collect information from a respondent. A questionnaire is typically a mix of close-ended questions and open-ended questions. Open-ended, long-form questions offer the respondent the ability to elaborate on their thoughts.

Advantages of the questionnaire technique are:

a) It is wide, simultaneous and relatively inexpensive sampling of opinion which can be conducted with reasonable effort;

b) Easy to summarize information from many sources

c) Questionnaires can be anonymous; therefore, their use is highly reasonable. However, the preparation of a good questionnaire requires the work of professionals who know how to prepare questions that can be understood and answered properly so the causes of specific deficiencies in performance can be assessed.

f) Problem analysis

Through the methods mentioned above, training requirements can be determined directly from the individuals involved. The problem analysis technique follows a more direct manner. Under this method, training needs can often be identified by an analysis of the problems which arise within an organization. Such analysis can be reports, written by an organization auditor or an external evaluator. There are many indicators which can be helpful in the investigation stage such as Client's complaints, Employee's failure to realize organizational difficulties, Poor communication in general, the activities of the organization are not very accessible to the public, the organization activities are weak etc. The existence of one or more of these problems can show evidence of the need for training. The problem may be rooted in several causes: one may be bad training or no training at all.

It is important therefore, to analyze the problem before prescribing the remedy. If there are, for example, lots of complaints from the clients about the service, the training requirement may be to tailor the course to serve the clients or customers (Customer care). If the problems are caused by lack of openness and awareness of the organization's activities, it may be responsible people to deal specifically with this. If employees have difficulty realizing plans or decisions, a training course for the manager geared to staff supervision is needed. It is also possible job descriptions may have to be changes and qualifications for the job are revised.

All these techniques will provide valuable data in assessing employee's performance. However, the limitations must also be considered. Since there are no perfect methods, it is highly recommended that a combination of methods is used followed by a comparison of data. Consistency in the results would suggest further evaluation was needed.

This can be archived through the use of questionnaires, organizing a training conference aimed at gauging group reactions or by discussion of the programme at the beginning of the training (training orientation). All forms of assessment by the respective groups are essential tools in planning programme.

For efficient performance of an organization, aspects like Knowledge, Attitude, Skills and Habits (KASH) are needed. Therefore, the following formula can be used to determine the Training Requirements/Needs. "KASH required *minus* KASH available *equals* Training Needs" (KR-KA=TNs).

Figure No. 8: Training Needs assessment formula

The above formula means that, the KASH available within an organization workers is compared to the requirements of the organization in terms of KASH, the gap is what is the training requirement.

Step 2: Defining Training Objectives

i) The importance of defining training objectives

After determining types, levels and amounts of training required, the next important step will be to define the training objectives. Through definition of objectives, it should become obvious what the training should achieve. If the training works, trainees will have achieved the objectives which had been set.

The definition of objectives is very important for the trainers because it determines the contents of the training. It also helps to decide which teaching procedure to follow and it enables the trainer to evaluate the efficiency of the training. It is important for the trainers, because it helps them to see what they can achieve from the training that they couldn't perform before. Generally speaking, defining objectives serves as a basis for establishing a training programme.

ii) The definition of the term training objectives

Before going further, it should be stated that aims and objectives are not the same. An aim is a general statement of intention, whereas a training objective is far more specific. The interrelation between aims and objectives are as follows:

While the aim is what will be the training impact, training objectives will be what the trainer wants the trainees to achieve at the end of a training. Similarly, the learning unit objective, is what will the trainees acquire from the training. A training and learning unit objective are the clear and precise statement of what the trainee will be able to do at end of the training and each learning unit.

However, Training objectives are of basic importance in all the stages leading to the formulation of a training course as well as in evaluating the effectiveness of the training.

This is because, training objectives are defined clearly and precisely in behavioral terms and the training objectives can be expressed on various levels i.e. the acquisition of knowledge, recognition and understanding, skills and abilities to take action and attitudes and valuations.

Preparation of training activities therefore, requires consideration of cognitive as well as the affective objectives of learning.

Step 3: Determining and Structuring the training Contents

While defining training objectives in step one above, the content of an activity was emphasized. Now, the content has to be determined in detail and arranged systematically in units.

In other words: we have to carefully plan the nature, amount and the structure of the subject matter to be taught.

a) Grading the subject

After determining the subjects in detail, it is advisable to "grade" the subject matter carefully to ensure the more essential ingredients of the training are communicated and understood within the time allocated for learning.

b) Structuring the subject

Once the content has been determined, it has to be systematically arranged according to certain criteria or principles. Content arrangement is necessary to make the material understandable. The content must be structured and cohesive in its presentation. The reaction and behavior of the participants must also be considered when developing a systematic structure. The trainer must consider ways to facilitate the transfer of the logical structure of the subject into the existing intellectual structure of the trainees.

In general, if the content is unstructured, the trainees will be more likely to forget what they learnt. Hence reinforcement depends on integration. The more meaningful and relevant a subject is, the more likely the trainees will remember it. Single, unconnected facts cannot be reproduced in the long run and requires the use of systematic thinking.

Following these criteria, the structure of a learning unit may have these different stages (section or phases)

Phase 1: Motivation Phase (Introduction – getting into the subject/topic)

A short introduction to the problem area should "warm-up" the trainees and should arouse their interest. The participants are confronted with a problem or task. They have to analyze the problem and, in some units, they can formulate the objectives. Usually a dialogue (a conversation) between trainer and participants will be the best method to utilize the knowledge and background of the participants. It is important to keep the interaction (conversation) relatively short to arouse the interest in what is to come without going too much in to detailed discussion. Without anticipating the statement about training aids, it should be clear that visualization of this introduction interaction can have a high motivating effect.

Phase 2: Intuitive Problem-Solving

Participants try to find solutions to the problem or they design plans or hypothesis for the learning points out difficulties, maybe directed by trainer who points out difficulties or gives a succession of learning steps, methods and aids (sources of information). As a result, the steps of learning or part objectives will be consolidated.

Phase 3: Appropriate problem-solving

By the time this stage is reached, the problem-solving should have been solved by effective working practices. It is during this phase that new and stimulating practical is presented. Traditionally, this is the stage where the trainer has a massive input but the participants should also be actively involved.

Step 4: Exercise and application (Consolidation)

The acquired knowledge has to be reinforced through repetition, memorizing or application. Participants should prepare short summaries or preset the concept of solution/rule in other ways. The use of notes as reinforcement method is very important. This can be achieved by: utilizing blackboard, transparencies, hand outs or working sheets. The importance of these reinforcers depends on arrows, underlining, framing important facts and using keywords. They are all better for developing logical thinking than presenting material in long sentences. Working in small group situations at this stage aids intensive consolidation.

Step 5: Review, Evaluation and Coda

Important parts of the learning unit should be reinforced and reflected upon because of their relationship to real life or work situations. This can be arranged in such a way that the participants become the initiators. The epilogue of this unit or lesson should pave the way for subsequent learning units or sequences.

In addition to these steps, organizers must carefully prepare all the facilities associated with training. Equipment, invitations, publicity, accommodation, meals and travel expenses are important to the success of the programme. Evaluation of the planned activities will be discussed prior commencing the training. At the end, the trainer needs to involve trainees to evaluate performance, thus gathering information and feedback which will be useful for future programmes.

Step 6: Selecting Appropriate Training Methods

When preparing the subject matter, the trainer is initially faced with the problem of having to decide which particular method or technique should be used. A survey of possible training methods, their characteristics, descriptions and special uses are given on the following table.

Table No. 16: Appropriate Training methods and their characteristics

TRAINING METOD	CHARACTERISTICS
Lecture method	Trainer/lecturer speaks (reads a paper) or displays on the board/projector and the participant listens

Discussion/debate method	Two or more participants talk together in a group, especially which the aim of convincing others of their own opinion
Moderation method	Trainer (Moderator) guides a group of experts (participants); he works within and amongst them; he helps to apply effective communication tools. The participants work in sub-groups and in plenary sessions.
Variants of Discussions: (Debates, Symposium, Colloquies)	A number of people and a moderator sit facing the audience discussing a topic. The audience can be passive (debate), put questions or give comments (symposium). If there is a real interchange of views between the experts and the audience, this is known as "colloquies."
Dialogue	A group of participants between two or more persons conversate and exchange of ideas with a view to reaching an amicable agreement or settlement. A facilitator can lead the conversation with guided principles basing on the issue in question.
Case Study	The participants receive a described situation (problem) which should be analyzed and solved. The results should be presented and discussed by a bigger group.
Demonstration	The Trainer explains or demonstrates a process or shows how an operation works
Question-answer technique	Trainer formulates questions, gives impulses, stimulates participants work alone or with a partner or in sub-groups of three to seven people to prepare answers.
Role-play	Participants (trainees) assume another identity and play a role and act out a conversation in a real-life situation. It is a game that shows real life within the target community. After the play, the observers (the other participants) give their resorts and a discussion will be started by the whole group.

Practical Exercise	Participants do something: they solve tasks, they apply rules, they use terms, they make use of presented solutions and strategies.
Training on the Job	The trainees work in a real job situation with instructor. Afterwards they demonstrate and explain the procedures, processes and operations. Sometimes, the trainees work as individuals or in small groups.

When presenting material in a lecture it is possible to get mental participation. The skilled trainer can apply the principle of "learning by doing" which involves challenging the trainees and allowing them time to think and present them with questions. However, it is important not to overload their concentration by appealing only to their sense of hearing.

Increasing participation by the trainees leads to a much stronger and more lasting impact. Experience through real life situations is the most effective form of learning. These facts are reinforced by the old saying: "If I hear it-I forget, If I see it-I remember, If I do it-I know it".

Figure No. 9: The value (%) in what people retain from learning

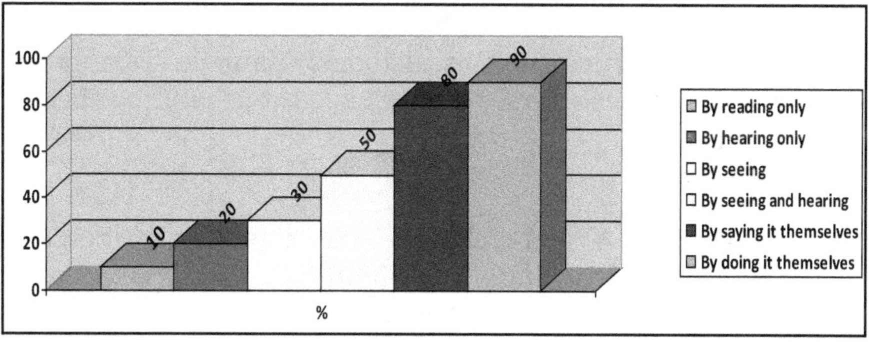

Learning by doing results in the highest level of retention, it is therefore extremely important. Self-involvement motivates people to learn more. However, "doing" doesn't just mean working with your hands. It should be understood that solving a problem intellectually is also "doing". In other words, "doing" can consist of answering questions, criticizing ideas, detecting ideas, analysis of written information, underlining important passages, writing down keywords, discovering connections, comparing, distinguishing, arranging, discovering connections and explanations, reporting and noting important terminologies, facts and rules.

Step 7: Design training aids and training materials

The objective of this step is to describe and illustrate the various types of training aids and materials as well as offering guidance on using them effectively. The fact that training methods, materials and aids are dealt with in different areas doesn't necessarily mean that there are clear distinctions and different preparation steps involved. Thinking about training methods includes thinking about materials and aids. The distinction was made in this book in an attempt to prepare better survey and clearer handling. It should however, be kept in mind that training methods have to be reinforced with well-prepared materials and aids. The following are some of information relating to training aids and materials.

1. **Written materials.** This includes; Manuals, Textbooks, Articles, Newsletters, Bulletins, information sheets, brochures, fliers, working papers and short summary papers.

2. **Visual Aids:** Visual techniques can significantly increase and reinforce learning. The planning and preparation of such aids requires time and imagination in the areas such as: selecting the points to be visualized, translating ideas into

positive visual forms, choosing the best medium, designing layout and choosing colors and evaluating effectiveness as an aid for future revision.

To put it generally: terms, diagrams, structures, concepts, formulas and summaries work better when presented on boards, charts or overhead projectors. Movements, flowing processes and the interrelationship of problems are best portrayed on flannel or magnetic boards.

Step 8: Work out a time-table/training schedule and training plan

The sequence of learning units is given through the systematic arrangement of the subject matter. However, in planning of the time-table, we have to consider some additional factors.

For the training to be effective, the participants need:

a) Variety; meaning alternations between large groups and small group situations, between information-gathering units, between talks, case studies, practical exercises and role-playing.

b) The trainees also need; a good pace, and,

c) a time for recreation.

Wherever possible, the least difficult unit should be taught first. The information-gathering units should generally precede the doing units to which they relate. However, it is not wise to teach too much theory before the trainees have had a chance to apply theory; they must get used to handling and solving problems first. Some activities have been designed so that all of the related theory just prior to the time it is needed by the trainee to solve practical problems. Where possible, information and theory should be administered in small doses throughout the training, seminar or course.

The training must be run at a pace which keeps everyone awake and interested, but which allows all participants to feel rewarded and successful. The experienced trainer should have acquired the knack of maintaining the right pace. But he has to be flexible; he has to monitor the reactions of the trainees and, if necessary, to increase or reduce the pace. However, if the time schedule is kept as flexible as possible, participants will have the opportunity to introduce units of their own into the programme. This can develop from questions raised and problems discussed by participants in small groups as they occur (ad-hoc small groups); or the discussions can be carried out over into plenary session.

As soon as the participants indicate their involvement by expressing a desire to influence the sequence of work, it is important that their initiative be taken up and included in the prepared programme.

Apart from good pacing and programme flexibility, it is necessary to set up an informal atmosphere in a pleasant learning environment which will stimulate participation and which will allow people to feel relaxed. The intense activity and extensive discussions require full attention and this is very hard work. In such circumstances, elements must be brought into the learning environment which have a soothing, cheering and re-vitalizing effect on the participant; music in the background during group work, perhaps. Sports and games are another way to re-vitalize the trainees after a long period of sitting. Relaxation, refreshment and outings such as coffee breaks can help create a climate more conducive to learning.

TRAINING/ TOPIC OBJECTIVE	MAIN TOPICS	SUB TOPIC	EXPECTED OUTPUT	FACILITATION METHODS TO BE USED	TIME FRAME (Minutes)
Stage Setting, motivation and Assessing Partici- pants' Compre- hension on the training	Stage Setting (Setting the mood for partici- pants full partici- pation)	Partici- pants' Introdu- ction	Motivated participants ready for training and confident towards a new situation	1. Fascinating introduction methods 2. Rolling ball 3. Singing/ Dancing 4. Role plays 5. Motivating images and/ or Slogan	15-20
	Assessing Partici- pants' expecta- tions	Focused questions e.g. what are expecta- tions	Participants' expectations revealed	Brainstor- ming	15-30
	Training objectives	Orientation on the training objectives	What is expected after the training	Clarification on the output of training Brainstor- ming	15-20
Promoting Awareness on the Concept of Partici- patory Planning in Develop- ment	Partici- patory Planning in Develop- ment (PPD)	Meaning, methods and Importance of PPD process	Knowledge and importance of PPD in development	1. Presentation 2. Focused open questions. 3.Q&A from both trainers and trainees	60

				1. Presentation 2. Focused open questions 3. Q&A from both trainers and trainees 4. Group work and presentations 5. Plenary discussion	
Orienting the Partici-pants on the Concept of Planning and Budgeting	Back-ground of Planning and Budgeting concept	Historical back-ground, definition, objectives, significance of planning and budgeting	Knowledge and understan-ding on the concept of planning and budgeting in development	1. Presentation 2. Focused open questions 3. Q&A from both trainers and trainees 4. Group work and presentations 5. Plenary discussion	60
Acquainting the Participants on Opportu-nities and Obstacles to Develop-ment (O&OD)	The concept of O&OD	Historical back-ground, definition, objectives and significance of O&OD system	Participants' knowledge, understan-ding and their ability to participate in O&OD process	1. Presentation 2. Focused open questions 3. Q & A from trainees and trainers 4. Group work and presentations 5. Plenary disc.	60
Assessing the training output	Training evaluation	Assessing if the training has met partici-pants expecta-tions	Training output assessed	1. Use of pre-prepared forms. 2. Brainstor-ming 3. Q&A	20-30

Table No. 17: Sample of a Training Plan

The amount of recreation time would of course depend on the duration of the training. A three-day seminar, for example, would not require the same recreation time as a course with intensive learning units. Each learning unit or session of 90 minutes should be followed by a break of 15 minutes. After one week of training, at least one day should be left free for recreation or an excursion.

In effect, schedules or time-tables can be precise and detailed while remaining flexible to the needs of the participants. The trainer should be ready to clear up participants' problems directly and should have time for unplanned activity.

Step 9: Arranging Training Facilities

Training has to be well organized. In addition to the subject matter, methods, materials and aids to be used, there are many other details and responsibly handled. Detailed organization will depend on local factors which cannot be described in this document. But remember, part of the job of a professional organizer is to follow certain procedures. This is called a checklist. A check list of a training programme will inform you about what has to be done, the facilities needed for the training, who is responsible to find/arrange them, the time frame with deadlines and the costs, if any.

Step 10: The Training schedule/agenda (Time table)

As it is in step 6, each training activity should be planned accordingly. Every trainer has to know the sequence flow of the training topics, time and methods to be used. The affective training however, should show the expected output of each topic, this will help the trainer and participants to measure if their expectations are met.

However, some practitioners do mix training schedule/ agenda with the training plan. While the training plan is the comprehensive flow of activities, the training programme will show just the topics, time and sometimes, the responsible trainer. The training plan includes many activities with a training activity being part of it.

REFERENCES AND BIBLIOGRAPHY:

✓ Agarwal (2001)

✓ Akhilesh G, (2019)

✓ Alexandra Cote (2019), *(Project Management Tools)*.

✓ Angualia, D. (2014) - *Legal Requirements for Registration of NGOs in Uganda*

✓ Brown, J. (2015), - *Top 4 Project Monitoring Steps.*

✓ Campbell P, (1988) – *Editorial ICA publications*

✓ Carrie Foster (2014), *Organization Development Practitioner; Consultant; Facilitator; Coach)*

✓ Chamala (1995:6)

✓ Chris's blog, (2009), *how to write a problem statement*

✓ Cook, C. R. (2005) - *Just enough project management.*

✓ CORAT Africa (2012) – *Leadership and Management Training manual*

✓ David Lornmen, (2016), - *Selected Top Secrets of Success for Managers and Leaders*

✓ ESAURP & ECD, (2009) - *CSOs Capacity Building Training Manuals*

✓ Estrella and Gaventa (1997)

✓ Eva Wieners, (2016), - *How to write a proposal*

✓ Francis et al (2012), - Creating Sense of Community: *The role of public space*

✓ Gerald Brooks (2008), - *Project Management Body of Knowledge*

✓ Grantsmanship Center (1993), *through ICA Belgium, ITPDP-1994 Training manual*

✓ Heathfield, S.M, (2020) – *What is Human Resource Development?*

✓ Hussein (1995),

✓ ICA Belgium, (1994), - *ITPDP Training Manuals*

✓ Kititz, N.J, (1974) - *Programme planning and proposal guide*

✓ Lane (1995)

✓ Libre, R. (2008), - *How to start a successful NGO in 10 steps*

✓ Margaret Rouse, (2014)

✓ Michener (1998)

✓ Mompati and Prinsen (2000)

✓ Muchunguzi D, (1995) - *Perspective*

✓ Mulder, P. (2018), - *SMART Goals. Retrieved (20th September 2019) from ToolsHero:*

✓ Mulder, P. (2018). *SMART Goals*

✓ Mulholland B, (2017)- *Six Types of Project Proposals That Get Approved*

✓ MyAccountingCourse.com (2020)

✓ Nyerere J.K. (1974), - *Man and Development*

✓ Otieno, F.A.O. (2000), – *The Role of Monitoring and Evaluation*

✓ Srinivas, H. (2015), – *Starting an NGO, Management Tools Series E-52*

✓ TRACE, (2006), - *Leading for improved Financial Management and Financial sustainability*

✓ URT (2002) - *The NGO Policy 2002*

✓ URT, (2002); T*he Non-Governmental Organization Act 2002*

✓ Valadez J, and Bamberger M, (1994), - *Monitoring and Evaluating Social Programs in Developing Countries*

✓ Vincent F, (1989*) - The manual of Practical Management*

✓ Vincent F, and Campbell P, (1989), - *Towards financial Autonomy*

✓ Vincent F, IRED. Geneva, (1989), - *Management Training Manual*

✓ Young D, (2017) - *Project Management*

IMPORTANT LINKS

- *(https://www.openpolytechnic.ac.nz/current-students/ study-tips-and-techniques/assignments/how-to-write-a-report/)*

- *.http://www.ngo.org/ngoinfo/define.html).*

- *http://int.search.myway.com/search/GGmain.jhtml/*

- *http://proposalsforngos.com/category/sample-proposals/*

- *http://proposalsforngos.com/category/sample-proposals/*

- *http://proposalsforngos.com/fund-raising-strategy/ how-not-to-impress-a-donor/*

- *http://vemmaattorneys.co.tz/2016/04/12/procedures-registering-international-ngos-tanzania/*

- *http://www.ceptara.com/blog/how-to-write-problem-statement*

- *http://www.fundsforngos.org/free-resources-for-ngos/ basic-questions-proposal-writing-answered/*

- *http://www.fundsforngos.org/free-resources-for-ngos/ difference-strategies-activities-proposal/*

- *http://www.fundsforngos.org/free-resources-for-ngos/proposal-writing-guidebook-grassrootsbased-ngoscboscsos/*

- *http://www.gdrc.org/ngo/start-ngo/index.html*

- *http://www.ngosindia.com/resources/ngo_registration1.php*

- <u>http://www.preservearticles.com/meaning/what-is-the-definition-of-the-term-organisation/29653</u>

- <u>http://www.tools4dev.org/resources/logical-framework-logframe-template/</u>

- <u>https://corporatefinanceinstitute.com/resources/knowledge/finance/cash-flow/</u>

- <u>https://en.wikipedia.org/wiki/Human_resource_management</u>

- <u>https://en.wikipedia.org/wiki/Logical_framework_approach/</u>

- <u>https://mail.google.com/mail/u/0/#search/funds+for+ngos/15599971257fb242/</u>

- <u>https://timelyapp.com/blog/project-monitoring-what-it-is-and-how-to-do-it-well</u>

- <u>https://www.fundsforngos.org/featured-articles/frame-goals-objectives-project-proposal/</u>

- <u>https://www.fundsforngos.org/free-resources-for-ngos/project-rationale-proposal/</u>

- <u>https://www.myaccountingcourse.com/accounting-dictionary/organizational-management</u>

- <u>https://www.openpolytechnic.ac.nz/current-students/study-tips-and-techniques/assignments/how-to-write-a-report/</u>

- <u>https://www.process.st/project-proposal/</u>

- <u>https://www.toolshero.com/time-management/smart-goals/</u>